EVERY PITCHER
TELLS A STORY

Letters Gathered by a Devoted Baseball Fan

SETH SWIRSKY

T I M E S **T** B O O K S

RANDOM HOUSE

All rights reserved under International and Pan-American Copyright
Conventions. Published in the United States by Times Books, a division
of Random House, Inc., New York, and simultaneously in Canada by
Random House of Canada Limited, Toronto.

Library of Congress Cataloging-in-Publication Data
Swirsky, Seth.
Every pitcher tells a story: letters gathered by a devoted baseball fan/by
Seth Swirsky.
p. cm.
Includes bibliographical references.
ISBN 0-8129-3055-X
1. Swirsky, Seth—Correspondence. 2. Baseball fans—United States—
Correspondence. 3. Baseball players—United States—Correspondence.
4. Pitchers (Baseball)—United States—Correspondence. I. Title.
GV865.A1S96 1999
796.357'092—dc21 99-19918

Random House website address: www.atrandom.com

Printed in the United States of America on acid-free paper.

98765432

First Edition

Design by Steven Brower

This book is dedicated with great love to my wife, Jody

Hi Julian

After reaching the mound, I couldn't remember if I ran there or if I flew there.
—Chan Ho Park

For the baseball fan, nothing is as interesting or more fun than hearing players recount their exploits in colorful detail with passionate intensity. And nothing is quite as amazing as the seemingly perfect recall they have about the day an exploit took place—not only the weather but the inning, the count, who was on which base, who was on deck, the score . . . every facet of the experience.

But the tales that pitchers tell stand out above those told by all other players. A pitcher stands alone on the mound, rapidly calculating the performance history of his opponent at the plate, deciding which kind of pitch to throw, assessing the defense behind him, and estimating the wisdom of the catcher's signal and target. All this in a few seconds that are deeply etched, for all time, in his memory. Indeed, those pitchers who do not develop the necessary memory skills soon find themselves in the minors or out of the game.

A pitcher is always thinking. Seeing the big picture. Telling the great story.

In my first book, *Baseball Letters: A Fan's Correspondence with His Heroes,* I wrote letters to hundreds of players asking questions about the part they played in baseball history, what they felt on momentous occasions, how they got their nicknames, or what circumstances placed them forever in the pantheon of baseball lore. Fueled by the enthusiastic response to the book and my ongoing love of the game, I decided to dive deeper into the game's rich history.

I read dozens of baseball books full of stories that stayed with me long after the books were closed. I wrote to approximately three hundred players, the famous and not so famous of yesterday and today. I received about two hundred replies. Among the 104 letters and documents in the book are letters from deceased ballplayers that I acquired. The letters from both the deceased and living ballplayers demonstrate the degree to which ballplayers have long seen themselves as the custodians of the game's history.

This book does not require the reader to have a

great knowledge of the game of baseball. It does ask the readers, however, to use their imaginations to transport themselves to the moment that each player wrote about. Some letters are long, some are short. Each, with the help of imagination, tells a story.

When my son, Julian, was born five years ago, I started collecting baseball memorabilia. It was thrilling to hold a baseball signed by the 1927 Yankees and to think to myself that Babe Ruth, Lou Gehrig, Leo Durocher, and others from that fabled team had held the same ball I was now holding. Wow . . .

Every night now before Julian goes to sleep he pleads, "Daddy, will you tell me a story?" I happily comply, then repair to my memorabilia room; I, too, want to be told a story.

Mixing the letters with many vintage photographs and many collectibles, I've tried to create a book reminiscent of a stroll through a museum, every page representing a different room to browse in and learn from.

Welcome to the 104 rooms of the museum! On the following walls (er, pages) are the works of Old Masters like Cy Young, Walter Johnson, Steve Carlton, Juan Marichal, and the "Dutch Master" Johnny Vander Meer, as well as many of their worthy successors, such as Roger Clemens, Pedro Martinez, David Cone, Tom Glavine, Kerry Wood, and Curt Schilling.

In addition, great sluggers add their observations about pitchers they've faced. Yes, the museum also includes the "works" of everyone from Reggie Jackson to "Shoeless Joe" Jackson, Jeff Bagwell, Rocky Colavito and ol' Zack Wheat. Some catchers, coaches, and commissioners are also represented. So sit back and enjoy the reminiscences of everyone from "The Rocket" to "The Space Man" to "Blue Moon". Your ticket has been stamped. Enjoy the exhibit!

May 1999

CONTENTS

EVERY PITCHER
TELLS A STORY

CARL PAVANO

Born 1976, New Britain, Connecticut. On the final game of the 1998 season, Carl, a promising rookie with the Montreal Expos, faced the game's human home-run-hitting machine, Mark McGwire. McGwire had shattered Roger Maris's thirty-seven-year-old record of 61 homers in a year—the game's most prestigious record—in early September, becoming baseball's all-time single-season home-run leader. Now, in the final at-bat of his inspiring season, with 69 home runs already to his credit (he had hit one earlier in the game off Pavano), "Big Mac" stood in to face the rookie again.

I ASKED CARL TO RECOUNT McGWIRE'S HISTORIC CLOUT.

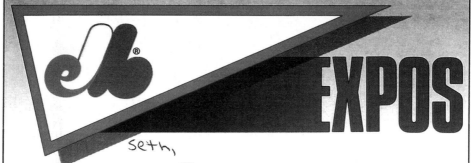

MONTREAL EXPOS

Seth,

In Response to your Letter, I am going to answer the question so many have asked. I knew it was the last game of the season and of my Rookie year with the montreal Expos. While sitting on the bench the previous 3 games against the Cardinals, I said to myself 'all along' if I get a chance to pitch against mcGuire, I will <u>not</u> walk him. I will <u>challenge</u> and <u>beat</u> him.'

First time in my Professional career going into a game as a Relief pitcher. He steps in as a I tow the rubber. A 3 to 3 tie with 2 outs in the bottom of the eigth with 2 men on. 52,000 people up on their feet cheering.

First pitch, CRACK-GONE, # 70

And the rest is History

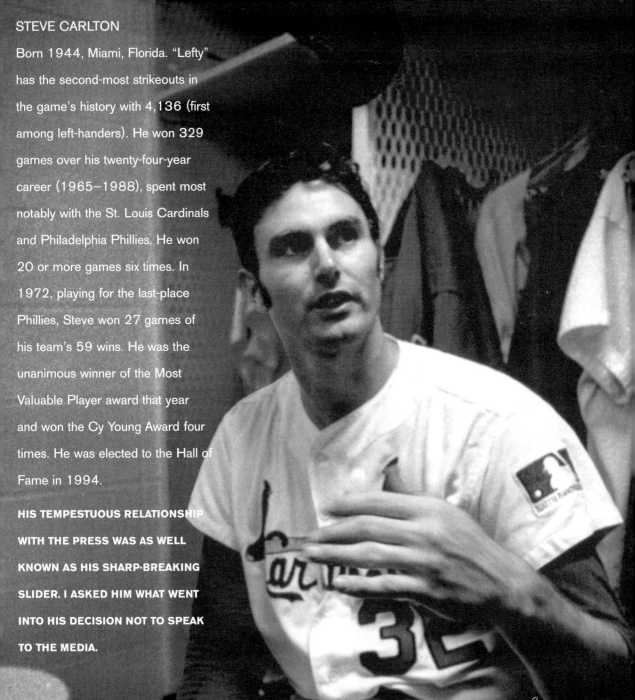

STEVE CARLTON

Born 1944, Miami, Florida. "Lefty" has the second-most strikeouts in the game's history with 4,136 (first among left-handers). He won 329 games over his twenty-four-year career (1965–1988), spent most notably with the St. Louis Cardinals and Philadelphia Phillies. He won 20 or more games six times. In 1972, playing for the last-place Phillies, Steve won 27 games of his team's 59 wins. He was the unanimous winner of the Most Valuable Player award that year and won the Cy Young Award four times. He was elected to the Hall of Fame in 1994.

HIS TEMPESTUOUS RELATIONSHIP WITH THE PRESS WAS AS WELL KNOWN AS HIS SHARP-BREAKING SLIDER. I ASKED HIM WHAT WENT INTO HIS DECISION NOT TO SPEAK TO THE MEDIA.

Dear Seth:

My decision not to speak to the media was not the result of any one incident. The media was crossing lines that had been drawn in baseball for many years. Reporting on the personal lives of players and breaking the trust that came with their access to the players. I felt it would be better for me and the fans if they covered me from the press box.

Looking back, I think that the writing was better and definitely more creative after I stopped speaking to the media.

Thanks for asking,

Steve Carlton

CHARLIE BROWN

I wrote to "Peanuts" creator Charles M. Schulz and asked him if Charlie Brown had ever pitched in front of his lifelong crush, the "little red-haired girl," and if it made him nervous. In response, I received a series of comic strips that ran in August 1968.

PEANUTS GOOD GRIEF, CHARLIE BROWN, WHEN ARE YOU GOING TO THROW THE FIRST PITCH?

THAT LITTLE RED-HAIRED GIRL IS WATCHING...I CAN'T LET GO OF THE BALL...MY FINGERS ARE NUMB

I'M STARTING TO SHAKE..LOOK AT ME! I'M SHAKING ALL OVER!

I DON'T SUPPOSE THERE'S A NEUROLOGIST IN THE STANDS..

WOULDN'T A GENERAL PRACTITIONER DO?

HOW ABOUT A VET?

PEANUTS COME ON, CHARLIE BROWN..WE'LL TAKE YOU HOME..

I'M GOING TO PITCH A GREAT GAME..

THAT LITTLE RED-HAIRED GIRL IS WATCHING, AND I'M GOING TO PITCH A GREAT GAME, AND SHE'S GOING TO BE IMPRESSED, AND...

WE'LL TAKE YOU HOME, CHARLIE BROWN, AND YOU CAN GO TO BED UNTIL YOU STOP SHAKING...

I'M GOING TO BE THE HERO AND PITCH A GREAT GAME AND THAT LITTLE RED-HAIRED GIRL WILL BE WATCHING AND I'LL BE PITCHING AND I'LL BE GREAT AND SHE'LL BE THERE AN..

PEANUTS OKAY, START THE GAME!

I FEEL BETTER! I'VE STOPPED SHAKING!

THE GAME'S OVER, CHARLIE BROWN, AND GUESS WHAT...**WE WON!**

LINUS TOOK YOUR PLACE...HE PITCHED A GREAT GAME...AND THERE WAS THIS LITTLE RED-HAIRED GIRL WATCHING...

SHE GOT SO EXCITED AFTER THE GAME THAT SHE RUSHED OUT TO THE MOUND, AND GAVE LINUS A BIG HUG!

AAUGH!

KERRY WOOD

Born 1977, Irving, Texas. The unanimous 1998 National League Rookie of the Year with the Chicago Cubs, Kerry has been heralded as baseball's next dominant power pitcher, in the Roger Clemens mold. He won 13 and lost 6 but, most impressively, held opposing hitters to a major-league-low .196 batting average. On May 6, he struck out twenty Houston Astros in one game, breaking Steve Carlton and David Cone's National League record of nineteen strikeouts and tying his idol Clemens's major-league mark for most strikeouts in a game.

AFTER KERRY'S HISTORIC GAME, CLEMENS CALLED HIM. I ASKED HIM WHAT "THE ROCKET" SAID TO HIM.

CHICAGO CUBS ───────────────

WRIGLEY FIELD

1060 W. Addison Street

Chicago, Illinois 60613-4397

773•404•CUBS

12/3/98

Seth,

The day after I struck out 20, I got a call from Roger. At first when I was told he was on the phone I thought it was a joke. And when I picked up the phone he said, "Hey Kerry this is Rocket, congratulations." I didn't know what to say. I had never met Roger, just talked a couple times on the phone, but still I was a little nervous.

He ~~just~~ just said that he was happy for me and proud to be sharing the record w/me. I met Roger for the first time in Orlando, at the Players Choice Awards. He ~~is~~ is a great person, has a wonderful family, and it was a honor to meet him. It's something I will never forget.

SINCERELY,

Kerry W

9

ROGER CLEMENS

Born 1962, Dayton, Ohio. Boston Red Sox, 1984–1995, Toronto Blue Jays, 1996–1998, New York Yankees, 1999– . He will surely go down as one of the greatest pitchers in the history of the game. His numbers and awards speak of his dominance: He is the only pitcher to win the coveted Cy Young Award for pitching excellence five times (1986, 1987, 1991, 1997, 1998); he was the 1986 American League Most Valuable Player; he shares the record for striking out the most hitters in one game with twenty (he's done it twice); he's had five twenty-win seasons. Over the past two seasons, at ages thirty-five and thirty-six, he has won 41, lost 13, and racked up 563 strikeouts in almost 500 innings (he has 3,153 career strikeouts). With a career 233–124 won-lost record and a 2.95 ERA, his place in Cooperstown is secure.

I ASKED ROGER WHO INSPIRED HIM TO GREATNESS GROWING UP AND WHO HE LEARNED THE MOST FROM ABOUT PITCHING DURING HIS CAREER.

11/21/98

SETH,

MY INSPIRATION GROWING UP WAS MY FAMILY. I COME FROM A LARGE FAMILY AND WATCHED HOW MY MOTHER AND GRANDMOTHER WORKED EXTREMELY HARD TO MAKE THE BEST OF EVERY SITUATION. I LEARNED NEVER TO BE SATISFIED WITH JUST OK, TO REACH FOR THE STARS.

PLAYING ON THE SAME TEAM AS TOM SEAVER WAS A THRILL FOR ME. I TRIED TO LISTEN CLOSELY WHEN HE SAID THINGS ON THE FIELD OR IN THE CLUBHOUSE. IT WAS ALSO INTERESTING WATCHING HIM SET UP HITTERS AT THAT STAGE OF HIS CAREER.

THE 1986 WORLD SERIES WAS BASEBALL AT IT'S BEST, AS WELL AS THE LCS SERIES. THERE IS NOTHING LIKE PLAYING BASEBALL IN LATE OCTOBER !

FINALLY, WINNING MY 5TH CY YOUNG WAS BOTH EXCITING AND HUMBLING. IT REALLY IS NICE TO BE COMPARED TO THE GREAT ONES WHO I'VE ALWAYS ADMIRED.

SINCERELY,
"ROCKET"

CY YOUNG

Born 1867, Gilmore, Ohio. Died Newcomerstown, Ohio, 1955. Hall of Fame, 1937. Between his first game in 1890 with the Cleveland Spiders and his last game with the Cleveland Indians in 1911, Denton True "Cyclone" Cy Young amassed a set of statistics that all rank first, all-time: 511 victories, 316 losses, 749 complete games, and 7,356 innings pitched. In five seasons he won more than 30 games, and he won 20 in ten others. He won more than 200 games in both the American and National leagues and was the first pitcher to throw a no-hitter in both leagues. He had seventy-six shutouts (fourth all-time) and once pitched twenty-four consecutive hitless innings over three games, which included the first perfect game in the American League (May 5, 1904). Cy once said, "Pitchers, like poets, are born, not made." He retired at age forty-four, because his expanding girth made it impossible for him to field bunts. Pitching's most prestigious honor—the Cy Young Award—was named after him in 1956.

IN THIS LETTER, WRITTEN TO A FAN IN FEBRUARY 1945, CY OFFERS HOMESPUN ADVICE ON HOW TO BECOME A PROFESSIONAL BASEBALL PLAYER.

Dear Sir—

Only way to learn this Game is to take lots of time. Play Ball as often as you Can—Pick out some spot you like in the game—that was the way i done. Then, get a chance for a try out. after you are serious you Can make the Grade.

i do not think you Can learn it overnight. you Can learn after 15 yrs. — 20 yrs. at least i learned till the End of My Career

Yours

Cy Young.

GARY KROLL

Born 1941, Culver City, California. Gary pitched for four teams in a four-year stint in the majors (1964–66, 1969). As a member of the New York Mets in 1965, he was the last man to start a game for the Mets before the Beatles played their infamous concert at Shea Stadium a few days later, on August 15, 1965.

I ASKED GARY IF HE REMEMBERS THE EXCITEMENT OF THE BEATLES COMING TO PLAY IN HIS HOME PARK.

Seth,

August 15 1965, Shea, the Beatles I was there, got to meet the Beatles. The atmosphere at the park that night was electrical hysteria, or better put a magical happening. It was the 60s it was new york it was the Beatles. a one time experience

Gary Kroll

This ball was signed by the Beatles the night of their historic concert at Shea Stadium.

Born 1909, North English, Iowa. On his fifth day in the major leagues, May 25, 1935, rookie pitcher Brown watched from the Pittsburgh Pirate bench as Babe Ruth, playing for the Boston Braves and eight days from retirement, hit the 714th and final home run of his titanic career. It was one of three homers Ruth hit that historic day.

I ASKED MACE WHAT HE REMEMBERED ABOUT BABE RUTH'S VERY LAST HOME RUN.

Seth:

After "Babe" Ruth hit his 3rd homer of the game, which cleared the roof of the double deck stand, he crossed home plate, and he run directly into _our_ dug out and sat right beside _me_ on the end of the bench! He sat there for about 4 or 5 minutes, right next to me. The only thing I remember him saying was, "Boy's that last one felt good"!

Sincerely,
Mace Brown

Babe Ruth, one more time

Cardinals, Al once stated, "When I'm on the road, my greatest ambition is to get a standing boo."

I WONDERED IF HE CREATED THE PERSONA OF THE "MAD HUNGARIAN" TO FRIGHTEN HITTERS AND WHETHER IT HURT HIS PITCHING WHEN CARDINAL MANAGER VERN RAPP MADE HIM SHAVE OFF HIS INFAMOUS MUSTACHE.

Mr. Swirsky

I developed my self psyche technique solely as a motivation for myself. This enabled me to have my "controlled hate mood" to destroy each batter. At the same time it took some hitters out of their mental approach to the game. Guys that would never step out of the batters box were stepping out trying to out psyche the master. They would try to out think me. As a result, I would be able to throw a pitch when their minds weren't completely focused on hitting. I have to much respect for my competitors to even think that I 'owned' anyone.

As to Mr. Vern Rapp and his 'no facial hair': No, I don't think Vern understood what my long hair and Fu Manchu meant to my psyche on the mound. Vern did not institute the rule to punish me, but as a result the mad Hungarian felt like a soldier going to war without his rifle!

Psyche up!

Al Hrabosky

The Mad
Hungarian

19

TURK WENDELL

Born 1967, Pittsfield, Massachusetts. Turk has compiled an 11–14 won-lost record with an impressive 3.29 ERA during his career spent with the Chicago Cubs (1993–1997) and the New York Mets (1997–present). A reliever with 27 career saves, he is one of baseball's more interesting characters; Turk has been known to brush his teeth between innings and also to wave to his outfielders while out on the mound.

PLAYERS USUALLY ONLY WANT TO RECOUNT THEIR MOMENTS OF GLORY ON THE FIELD. BUT I WANTED TO KNOW FROM TURK IF HE WOULD SHARE HIS MOST EMBARRASSING MOMENT IN BASEBALL.

"GOT ON THE THRONE"

DURING THE 1996 SEASON, AS I PLAYED FOR
THE CHICAGO CUBS, I GOT INTO A DAILY ROUTINE.
THIS WENT FROM THE TIME I GOT TO THE
BALLPARK, RIGHT UP TO THROWING MY WARM-UPS
TO GO INTO THE GAME.
THE ROUTINE WAS THAT I ALWAYS USED THE RESTROOMS
DURING THE FIFTH INNING.

WE WERE PLAYING THE L.A. DODGERS IN
L.A., AND IT WAS A DAY GAME. THAT MEANT
WE OCCUPIED THE RIGHT FIELD GRAND STANDS.

WELL, WHEN THE FIFTH INNING ROLLED AROUND I
INFORMED ALL MY BULLPEN MATES, AND COACH DAVE BIALAS
THAT I'D BE IN THE BATHROOM. THEY ALL
ACKNOWLEDGED WHERE I'D BE AS I DEPARTED.

THERE I SAT ON THE "OL MIGHTY" PORSOLIN (SP)
GOD" WHEN DAVE OPEN THE DOOR THE BULLPEN
RESTROOM WIDE OPEN! EVERYONE IN THE GRANDSTAN
LAUGHED, AND STARTED WAVING TO ME.

WELL, BEING LITTERALY CAUGHT WITH MY PANTS
DOWN, I COULD DO NOTHING BUT WAVE BACK.

DAVE APOLOGIZED UP AND DOWN AND SHUT
THE DOOR AND QUICKLY AS HE COULD, BUT THE
DAMAGE WAS DONE!

WHEN I WAS DONE I OPENED THE DOOR
AND THE CROWD ROARED, LAUGHED, AND WAVED
AGAIN! WHAT AN EMBARRASSMENT!

TURK WENDELL

JEFF BAGWELL

Born 1968, Boston, Massachusetts. "Bags" is one of the National League's premier power hitters of the 1990s. He was named Rookie of the Year in 1991 and Most Valuable Player in 1994. He's been the main ingredient in the Houston Astros' attack since he was traded to them by the Red Sox in 1990. Overcoming many hand injuries, he continues to be a major force at the plate with 221 career home runs.

SINCE HE'S SUCH AN ASTUTE OBSERVER OF THE GAME, I WAS INTERESTED IN KNOWING WHAT JEFF'S IMPRESSIONS WERE OF PITCHERS AS A GROUP.

Seth,

Pitchers, as a group, are generally strange. They have different opinions of the game than the every day to day players.

Starting pitchers spend 4 days not paying attention to the game, and on the 5th day, their start, they have no idea whats going on. You generally find the best pitchers in the game pay attention more consistently then others.

Relief pitchers are more in tune with situations in the game because their roles are more similar to the every day player.

Despite an every day players perspective, the game couldn't be played without pitchers.

Sincerly, Jeff Bagwell

HOUSTON ASTROS BASEBALL CLUB
P.O. BOX 288 • HOUSTON, TEXAS 77001-0288 • 713-799-9500
BASEBALL ADMINISTRATION FAX 713-799-9562 • MARKETING FAX 713-799-9794 • TICKET SERVICES FAX 713-799-9812

NATIONAL LEAGUE WEST CHAMPIONS
1980   1986

NATIONAL LEAGUE CENTRAL CHAMPIONS
1997   1998

CURT SCHILLING

Born 1966, Anchorage, Alaska.
Curtis Montague Schilling's
game is pure power baseball. He
throws lots of hard fastballs simply
challenging the batter to hit them.
Most can't. A ten-year veteran
(Baltimore Orioles, 1988–90,
Houston Astros, 1991,
Philadelphia Phillies, 1992–
present), he has led the National
League the past two seasons with
619 strikeouts. With a little run
support Curt would be a consistent
20-game winner.

**I ASKED HIM WHAT GOES THROUGH
HIS MIND IN THE HOURS BEFORE
HE TAKES THE MOUND. CURT
RESPONDED BY E-MAIL.**

Date: Friday, May 29, 1998 5:49: 42 AM
From: Curt Schilling
Subj: Re: Got your note-thanks
To: PS72907@aol.com

Seth,

I can't divulge alot, but one of the overriding and prevelant thoughts in my mind as I drive to the park, and it may sound weird, is realizing I'm about to pitch in a big league game, gives me goose bumps every fifth day and always seems to work!

Gameday for me starts when I wake up. I don't wake up at any set time unless it's a day game, but I try to get a solid nights sleep so I can ease into the day when I wake up.

What superstitions I do have mostly revolve around food and times on the day I pitch with the first being lunch. I eat a certain type and brand of frozen pizza every day of a home game that I am pitching, my son Gehrig usually has a slice with me. Why? 'Cause it has worked to this point.

I leave at exactly the same time EVERY game, arriving usually around a 20 or 15 minute window, gotta account for bad traffic. I arrive early enough to allow myself time to settle in at the park. I live 45 minutes from the stadium so the drive in allows me to slip into a very good frame of mind for the night.

Ballpark routine is exact, to the minute, every single time. Pre-game video with Vuk, BP, stretch, pre-game meeting with Vuk, Lieby and Galen and then to the dugout and finally the pen. Warmups begin exactly the same time prior to every game I pitch, first toss of warmups comes 20 minutes before home game, 15 for a road game, this is preceded 5 minutes by short sprints with Bernie to get a good blood flow and start the BP rising.

Then it's gametime.
Curt Schilling

WARREN BUFFETT

Born 1931, Omaha, Nebraska.
According to *Forbes* (June 1998),
Warren is the second-wealthiest individual in the world. His actions and
transactions move world markets.
He also happens to be the pitcher on
his Berkshire Hathaway company's
hardball team, known as Warren
"The Whip."

**I ASKED HIM IF HE SEES PARALLELS
BETWEEN BASEBALL AND STOCK
PICKING.**

WARREN E. BUFFETT, CHAIRMAN

August 26, 1997

Mr. Seth Swirsky
November Nights Music Inc.

Dear Seth:

Thanks for your note. I'm enclosing a copy of Berkshire's 1994 Annual Report where on page five I analogize between our business and investment style and the approach of Ted Williams to hitting.

A few weeks ago, I watched Tony Gwynn and Ted on The Classic Sports Network where he talked of his book, *The Science of Hitting.* I then obtained a copy, which had a diagram prepared by Ted showing what his batting average would be if he swung at balls in various parts of the strike zone. If he waited for a pitch in his "happy zone," he was a .400 hitter; if he swung at one in the lower outside section of the strike zone, his average would be more like .260. This "wait for the fat one" approach is right on the money in terms of making investment decisions, and I may write more about it in next year's report.

A major advantage in investing, however, is that there is no such thing as a called strike. In money-management, the crowd can be screaming "Swing you bum," but even if the pitch is right down the middle, you can wait all day for one that is just a fraction more to your liking. Only if you swing and miss an "investing pitch" is there a penalty. This "no-called strike" aspect to investing is a huge advantage for the patient investor.

Best regards.

Sincerely,

Warren E. Buffett

WEB/db
Enclosures

27

CHAN HO PARK

Born 1973, Kong Ju City, South Korea. A top right-handed starter with the Los Angeles Dodgers (1994–present), Chan Ho was the first Korean to play major-league baseball when he took the mound on April 8, 1994.

LOS ANGELES

I ASKED HIM IF HE HAD FUN IN HIS FIRST MAJOR-LEAGUE GAME. HE ANSWERED IN BOTH KOREAN AND ENGLISH.

1000 ELYSIAN PARK AVENUE
LOS ANGELES, CA 90012-1199

나의 첫 메이져 리그 등판때의 상황과 기분은 이렇다. 역대 메이져 리그사상 17 번째로 마이너 리그를 거치지 않고 메이져 리그로 직행하는 선수가 되었다. 꿈을 이룬것 같았던 그때의 기분은 말로 표현할수 없었다.

'94年 4月 8日 이었을 것이다. Atlanta Braves 와의 경기였다. 지고 있었던 경기의 9회 마지막 이닝을 내가 던지기 위해 불펜에서 몸을 풀고, 불펜에서 마운드 까지 달려가는 그때 나의 기분은 지금도 기억이 생생하다. 뛰어 가면서 다리에 전혀 느낌이 없었고 느껴 볼래야 느낄수 없었던 것은 너무나 흥분되고 긴장된 약 1분동안의 긴장 이었다. 더욱이 내가 마운드 까지 향하는 동안 5만여명의 관중들은 모두 일어서서 나에게 박수를 치고, 알아들을수는 없었지만 내게 환호성을 질러 댔다. 그래서 더욱 흥분했었고, 마운드까지 뛰어 갔는지 날아 갔는지 분간 할수조차 없었다.

나는 한이닝동안 두개의 꼴볼과 하나의 안타를 허용하고 2실점을 했으나 두개의 삼진도 잡아냈다. 비록 좋지 않은 성적으로 끝낸 이닝 이었지만 관중들은 역시 모두일어나서 내게 격려와 축하의 박수를 보내 주었다.

이렇게 해서 보낸 나의 첫 메이져리그 등판은 영원히 잊을수 없는 나의 추억이 되었다.

8-31-98

LOS ANGELES **Dodgers**®

1000 ELYSIAN PARK AVENUE
LOS ANGELES, CA 90012-1199

This is how I remember my Major League debut. In baseball's history, I was the 17th person to go directly into the Majors without previous experience in the minor leagues. It was a dream come true for me and no words could express how I felt at that moment.

April 8, 1994. It was a game against the Atlanta Braves. I can vividly remember running out to the mound, when we were down against the Braves in the 9th inning, after preparing myself in the bullpen. I couldn't feel my legs when I was running out to the mound due to the excitement and tension that gave me the shivers for about a minute. 50,000 fans stood up and cheered me on while I was heading for the mound and although I couldn't understand what they were saying, the one thing I knew was they were cheering for me. This built up the excitement in me even more and after reaching the mound, I couldn't remember if I ran there or if I flew there.

I pitched for an inning and gave up two walks, a hit, and two earned runs but I did strike out two. Although I had a poor performance in that one inning, the fans at the stadium nevertheless stood up and clapped with acceptance. Because of this, I will never forget my memorable debut in the Major Leagues.

August 31, 1998
Chan Ho Park

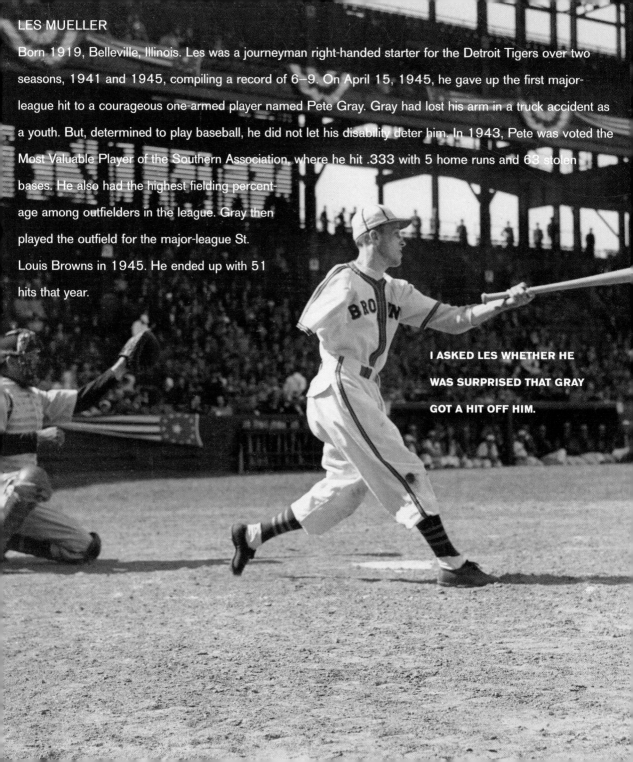

LES MUELLER

Born 1919, Belleville, Illinois. Les was a journeyman right-handed starter for the Detroit Tigers over two seasons, 1941 and 1945, compiling a record of 6–9. On April 15, 1945, he gave up the first major-league hit to a courageous one-armed player named Pete Gray. Gray had lost his arm in a truck accident as a youth. But, determined to play baseball, he did not let his disability deter him. In 1943, Pete was voted the Most Valuable Player of the Southern Association, where he hit .333 with 5 home runs and 63 stolen bases. He also had the highest fielding percentage among outfielders in the league. Gray then played the outfield for the major-league St. Louis Browns in 1945. He ended up with 51 hits that year.

I ASKED LES WHETHER HE WAS SURPRISED THAT GRAY GOT A HIT OFF HIM.

12-2-97

Dear Seth,

I Did Admire Pete. Gray as I am Sure most Players Did. He Played Very Well Considering His Handicap & I Was most Shocked That He Got a Hit — But Let me Tell you I really Was Shocked When He Just missed By a Few Feet of Hitting a Home Run off me in another Game, I came in relief Late In The Game with several men on Base & He Put Our Right Fielder in Detroit up Against The Wall & Just Gave me a Save in That Game, so I Almost Gave Him His First & Only Homer in the Big Leagues Ha!

Best Wishes,
Lee Mueller

JERRY REUSS

Born 1949, St. Louis, Missouri. Jerry is the fifth-winningest left-hander in National League history with 220 wins. He was a rare four-decade player (1969–1990), pitching for eight teams, including the Los Angeles Dodgers and the Pittsburgh Pirates. He once said: "If I had a shortstop with a twenty-five-foot wingspan, who could leap twenty-five feet in the air, all my problems would be solved."

I WONDERED IF, WHEN HE SEES HIS OLD TEAMMATES AFTER MANY YEARS, IT'S JUST LIKE "OLD TIMES" OR HAVE THINGS CHANGED.

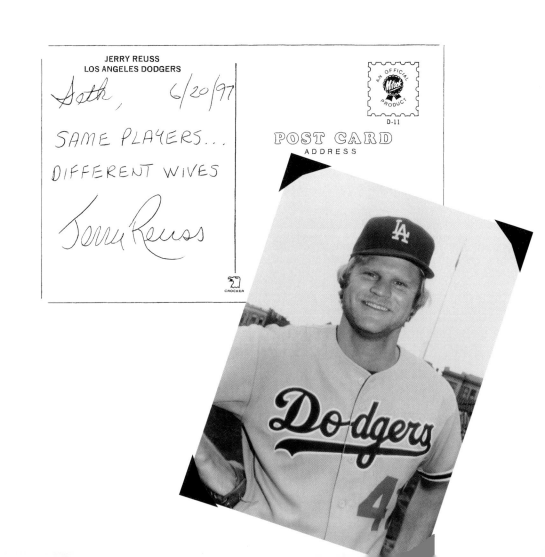

JERRY REUSS
LOS ANGELES DODGERS

Seth,   6/20/97

SAME PLAYERS...
DIFFERENT WIVES

Jerry Reuss

POST CARD
ADDRESS

KEN KRAHENBUHL

Born 1968, Oxnard, California. On July 23, 1998, Ken was traded from the Pacific Suns to the Greenville (Mississippi) Bluesmen of the Western Baseball League, not for another player, but for ten pounds of catfish. (The year before, the Bluesmen had acquired their second baseman in a trade for a box of Muddy Waters blues records.) In Ken's first game with his new team he pitched a perfect game.

I WONDERED WHAT WAS THE WORST AND BEST THING ABOUT BEING TRADED FOR A BUCKET OF FISH.

Greenville Bluesmen **Professional Baseball Club**   601-335-BLUE

1040 South Raceway Rd.   Greenville, MS 38703   Fax (601) 335-7742

Having to explain to friends and family that you were traded for fish is the most humiliating thing I had ever done. Throwing a perfect game the next day was the most satisfying.

In my 8yr minor league career I never thought being traded for catfish would bring me so much attention, but it has. A perfect game is a great milestone in any pitchers career but it was 10 pounds of catfish that brought me fame. All the attention has giving me many opportunitys I may have never gotten especially to a guy who has had 4 elbow surgerys. Baseball is truely a funny game

"Catfish"

ROCKY COLAVITO

Born 1933, New York City. Getting traded is the most shocking event that can happen in a player's career.

On the day before the 1960 season was to begin, Cleveland Indian Rocco Domenico "Rocky" Colavito, one

of the game's most feared sluggers (374 home runs) when he played from 1955 to 1968, was traded to

the Detroit Tigers for singles hitter Harvey

Kuenn. The trade shocked the baseball world

and horrified Indian rooters who loved

Colavito. Indian fans would never forgive

General Manager "Trader" Frank Lane for

the move. Rocky was later traded back to the

Indians late in his career.

Known as a strong-armed outfielder, Rocky also

made two major-league pitching appearances. All

told, he gave up five walks while striking out two in

5.2 innings, earning one win.

I ASKED ROCKY WHAT HE FELT WHEN HE FIRST

FOUND OUT HE WAS TRADED AND IF HE EVER ASKED

"TRADER" LANE WHY HE WAS DEALT.

8-21-97

Dear Seth,

    To Answer your question, <u>Shock</u>" Total shock
I was told while I was the baserunner at first base
in the last spring training game traveling north,
in Memphis, Tennessee. Joe Gordon approached me
and said 'Rocky thats the last time you will
bat as a Cleveland Indian, you've been traded to
the Detroit Tigers for Harvey Kuenn.'
    I saw Frank Lane many times after the
trade. I cant think of anything nice to say
about him so I wont say anything at all.
        Sincerely,

P.S. Gordon was wrong!   Rocky Colavito

PETE HARNISCH

Born 1966, Commack, New York. One of the game's elite starters, Pete has pitched for Baltimore (1988–1990), Houston (1991–1994), the New York Mets (1995–1996), and the Cincinnati Reds (1998–present). He took off the 1997 season, battling depression. He came back strong with the Reds in 1998, posting a 14–7 won-lost record, boosting his career mark to 86–84, with a 3.79 ERA.

I ASKED PETE IF HIS YEAR OFF GAVE HIM A DIFFERENT PERSPECTIVE ON THE GAME, AND IF THAT ULTIMATELY MADE HIM A BETTER PITCHER.

THE CINCINNATI RED

REDS est. 1869

100 Cinergy Field   Cincinnati, OH 45202   513 421 4510
tlx: 513 421 REDS   fax: 513 421 7342   www.cincinnatireds.com

12/11/98

I DON'T KNOW IF IT MADE ME A BETTER PITCHER, BUT I DO KNOW THAT IT PUT LESS IMPORTANCE ON THE OUTCOME OF GAMES. PERSPECTIVE IS A WONDERFUL THING. BEING AWAY WHEN I WAS SICK DID TWO THINGS; 1) RE-EMPHASIZED THE IMPORTANCE OF FAMILY AND <u>REAL</u> FRIENDS!

2) PUT INTO PERSPECTIVE THE IMPORTANCE OF BASEBALL IN MY LIFE. (IT'S A SMALL PERCENTAGE BUT SOMETIMES THAT GETS LOST WHEN YOU'RE PITCHING POORLY!

TO SUMMARIZE, MY BEING AWAY FROM THE GAME PUT THE GAME INTO PERSPECTIVE. IF YOU WORK VERY HARD TO BE IN EXCELLENT PHYSICAL SHAPE AND BE PREPARED TO PITCH THAN IT'S ALL YOU CAN DO. GIVE 100% AND ACCEPT THE RESULTS. A VALUABLE LESSON I'M JUST NOW STARTING TO LEARN!!!

[signature]

National League Champions: 1919 - 1939 - 1940 - 1961 - 1970 - 1972 - 1975 - 1976 - 199'
World Series Champions: 1919 - 1940 - 1975 - 1976 - 1990

DETROIT TIGERS, INC.
2121 TRUMBULL AVENUE
DETROIT, MI 48216
(313) 962-4000

JUSTIN THOMPSON

Born 1973, San Antonio, Texas. A
talented young left-hander, Justin is
the ace of the rebuilding Detroit
Tigers team of the late 1990s.

I ASKED HIM WHAT KIND OF PRES-

SURE GOES WITH BEING NAMED A

NUMBER-ONE STARTER.

Seth

It's a honor to be named a #1
starter. A lot of expectations come with the role because
your team expects you to go out there every five days and
give them a strong performance. The way I look at the
situation is that it's a great challenge because you always
face other teams #1 starters which means a lot of times
your not going to get the run support. So when you get
a couple of runs you really got to bear down and show
them why you are a #1 starter. It definitely is
one of the most challenging tasks that I have every
tried but I also wouldn't change it for the world.

Just Thompson

WORLD CHAMPIONS

CARL MAYS

Born 1891, Liberty, Kentucky. Died 1971, El Cajon, California. A spitballer, Carl pitched from 1915 to 1929 with the Boston Red Sox, New York Yankees, Cincinnati Reds, and New York Giants. With a career record of 208 wins and 126 defeats (.622 winning percentage), five seasons winning 20 or more games, and a lifetime 2.92 earned run average, he would have been a lock for the Baseball Hall of Fame, if not for one unfortunate pitch he threw in the fifth inning of a game against the Indians on August 16, 1920. That pitch struck Cleveland's beloved shortstop Ray Chapman on the head. Chapman died less than a day later from the injury. Coincidentally, he and Chapman were born the same year, a mile apart from each other. Mays was unfairly vilified as the only pitcher in major-league history to kill a man. The Hall of Fame's Veterans Committee might want to seriously consider an exceptional player whose involvement with baseball's most tragic event was purely unintentional.

THE NEARLY EIGHTY-YEAR-OLD MAYS WROTE THE FOLLOWING LETTER TO A FRIEND. IT IS THE ONLY KNOWN ACCOUNT BY MAYS OF HIS ROLE IN THE DEATH OF RAY CHAPMAN.

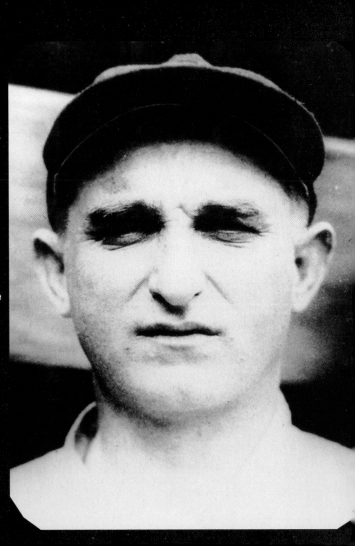

Ive had to live with this thing with hitting Chatman. The papers said I was guilty and the general public believes everything they see in the paper.

Chatman was hit because when he shifted his back foot we all knew he was going to push the ball down the first base line, if he did no one could throw him out, he was so fast, So we would bring the ball <u>up</u>, to try to make him pop it up, So he ran into a high pitch, <u>over the plate</u> — Please make a mental picture of this for me.

it would be my first
and last request—the
the umpire said in all the
papers, "the Ball was over
the plate high"— Huggins
fined me. Every word of this
is true.

I've never been very
lucky, and I blame
the most of it on lack of
education, which I wanted
more than anything, but it
was denied me, no Father,
no money, Country school,
and had to stay home to
help feed the family.

Lots of Love
Carl

The petition
the stunned
Indians players
signed follow-
ing the death
of their beloved
shortstop

BOSTON, August 24, 1920.

Mr. B. B. Johnson, Pres. American League

Dear Sir.

WE, THE UNDERSIGNED, members of the Cleveland
Base Ball Club, have resolved to take no part in any ball
game in which Mr. Carl Mays shall take part.

We will also back any similar action taken by
the members of any other American League Club.

A copy of this action is being sent to the
players of every club, also a copy to Mr. B. B. Johnson.

Signed:

Joe Evans

Ray Caldwell

George Burns

O. Thomas

Guy Morton

Wm. Wambsganss

Harry Lunte

Elmer J. Smith

J. Bagby

Chas Jamieson

Joe Wood

L. G. Nunamaker

John D. Brancey

Ed Ellison

Wm. Johnston

Jack McCalbster

Stanley Coveleski

Robt. W. Clark.

W. L. Gardner.

Steve O'Neill.

Ray Chapman (doffing his cap)

Trailblazers: From left, Roy Campanella, Larry Doby, Don Newcombe, Jackie Robinson

DON NEWCOMBE

Born 1926, Madison, New Jersey. "Newk" pitched most notably for the Brooklyn Dodgers (1949–1951, 1954–1957) before finishing up with the Reds and Indians. He is the only pitcher in the history of baseball to win the Rookie of the Year award (1949), along with the Cy Young Award (1956) and the Most Valuable Player award (1956). He was the ninth African-American player to play in the major leagues, following in the footsteps of Jackie Robinson, Larry Doby, Hank Thompson, Willard Brown, Dan Bankhead, Roy Campanella, Satchel Paige, and Minnie Minoso. **I ASKED HIM HOW FAR HE FELT RACE RELATIONS HAD COME IN BASEBALL SINCE THOSE EARLY DAYS OF INTEGRATION.**

Dear Seth,

We have come a long way in race relations since Jackie Robinson, Roy Campanella, Larry Doby and myself first came on the baseball scene, however there still is a long way to go. For example: We all can live and eat with our teammates now, but in my era that wasn't possible in some of our American cities, and I've always asked Why? We could fight and die for our country when necessary, but we could not stay at the same hotel. We could pay our taxes if we had a lot of some sort, but we could not play baseball except when you were separated.

Jackie Robinson helped to change all that, but a white man had to give him a chance first. So, I'll be forever endebted to Branch Rickey for my chance, but Jackie Robinson was the inspiration that young kids as I need to succeed in our country today and now that chance is available to them. So Yes, we've come a long way in all this, but the struggle, and it was a struggle is far from over, overall.

As ever
Don Newcombe

DAVID CONE

Born 1963, Kansas City, Missouri. One of baseball's premier strikeout artists during his career (1986–present) spent with the Royals, Mets, Blue Jays, and Yankees, Cone has compiled a career 168–93 won-lost record, winning the 1994 Cy Young Award. In 1991, he struck out nineteen Phillies to tie what was then the National League mark.

An intelligent pitcher, keeping batters off balance by throwing from various arm angles, he was one of the 1998 Yankee mainstays in their march to become baseball's winningest team in history.

I WONDERED IF HE THOUGHT THE '98 YANKS WERE THE GREATEST EVER AND WHAT MADE THE TEAM SO SPECIAL.

A season to remember; the Yankees celebrate their world series victory over the Padres, 1998.

New York Yankees

TICKET OFFICE
YANKEE STADIUM
BRONX, NEW YORK 10451
(718) 293-6000

EXECUTIVE OFFICE
YANKEE STADIUM
BRONX, NEW YORK 10451
(718) 293-4300

12-4-98

Dear Seth -

Are we the greatest team of all time? How does one make comparisons that span decade upon decade?

After losing three out of our first four games, the 1998 New York Yankees went 149-46 to finish with a 125-50 record of historical proportions.

The numbers are staggering but the attitude and professionalism of the Yanks are even more impressive.

There were major contributions from all corners of the clubhouse that help create an atmosphere of selflessness and depth the likes of which are arguably unparalleled in the history of BASEBALL. This team gave NEW MEANING to the old cliche, "The sum is greater than it's parts." NOT ONE PLAYER stood head AND shoulders ABOVE ANY other. FROM pitching AND Defense, to speed AND power, All of the BASES WERE LITERALLY COVERED.

ONE must Also CONSIDER A team that DISPLAYED INCREDIBLE HEART AND CHARACTER that evolved from some of the most compelling human interest STORIES EVER WITNESSED AND COVERED IN New York Sports history.

I SAY It's AN honor for US to be mentioned in that Context AND I hope the great Debate goes ON AND ON AND ON. It seems to me that this is how Legends AND Legendary teams ARE MADE.

Sincerely — '98
David Cone YANKS

WALTER "DUTCH" RUETHER

Born 1893, Alameda, California. Died 1970, Phoenix, Arizona. Dutch pitched with four teams during an eleven-year career that lasted from 1917 to 1927. A winner of 137 games, he was a valuable contributor on his last team, the glorious 1927 Yankees. Many believe that Murderer's Row, led by Babe Ruth, Lou Gehrig, and other "windowbreakers," was the best baseball team in history. **ALTHOUGH DUTCH DID NOT GET TO SEE THE 1998 YANKEES, HE IS ADAMANT ABOUT WHO THE GREATEST TEAM EVER WAS.**

In the 1st place dont try to compare any of the modern day ball club to the 1927 Yankees — There is no comparison. The 27 Yankee would win either pennant National or American league by at least 30 games.

Babe Ruth had to be the most ~~vaut~~ valuable player on any club.

The most underrated player I would say was Mark Koenig

My contribution was 13 Games won & 6 lost by the 1st of August. I did not pitch another inning all year on account of a suit I had filed against the Hearst publications.

Hope this helps a little.

Walter "Dutch" Ruether

ELIAS SOSA

Born 1950, La Vega, Dominican Republic. In the sixth game of the 1977 World Series, New York Yankee outfielder Reggie Jackson hit three home runs on three consecutive pitches off three different Los Angeles Dodger pitchers. Sosa, a solid reliever with eight different teams (1972–1983), was Jackson's second victim that electric night in New York City.

I ASKED ELIAS WHAT IT FELT LIKE TO FACE THE FEARSOME JACKSON.

I felt butterflies in my stomach facing R.J. in the 1977 World Series as I ran from the bullpen to the pitching mound, knowing that Yankee Stadium was jam-packed.

The scouting report on R.J. was to stay hard up and in with a good fast-ball. I don't have any regrets about that pitch. My catcher Steve Yeager came to the mound and said, "he hit a very good pitch".

Whether he was guessing or not, I have to give him credit. I went out and did exactly what I was supposed to do. Even though the result was negative.

Elias Sosa

, Wyncote, Pennsylvania. Reggie played for twenty one years (1967–1987) most notably wi

letics, New York Yankees, and California Angels. He hit 563 career home runs (sixth all-time)

ue four times. In 1973, he was named the American League's Most Valuable Player. His team

ive World Series they played in, and his .755 Series slugging percentage was the highest eve

to the Hall of Fame in 1993.

uckleballer Charlie Hough was Reggie's third victim in his three-home run barrage during the s

1977 World Series. It was those home runs that forever endowed Reggie with the name "Mr

I WONDERED WHAT REGGIE RECALLED ABOUT FACING HOUGH.

The Mr. October Foundation for Kids

October 22, 1997

Seth Swirsky
November Nights Music Inc.

Dear Seth,

Thank you for your letter.
Your question pressed the "way back button" but it is a memory that always brings pleasant thoughts. As you know Charlie Hough was a knuckleball pitcher and throughout my career had success off knuckle ball pitchers. Being a baseball fan you will remember the Chicago White Sox pitcher, Wilbur Wood, a knuckle baller, who let's just say I was very fortunate when hitting against him. I always felt confident against knuckle ball pitchers. When I saw Charlie Hough start the inning, did I know I was going to hit a home run? Obviously, my confidence was sky high, I thought my chances *might* be pretty good. The scouting report on Hough was that he liked to "start off" with his knuckleball. I was just praying it would be "something to hit." You know the rest of the story!

Your letter touched my heart, again, thank you.

Sincerely,

Reggie Jackson
a.k.a. "Mr October"

The third home-run ball

Born 1945, New York City. Jim was the best right-handed hurler in the American League during a career (1965–1984) spent entirely with the Baltimore Orioles. He was a three-time winner of the Cy Young Award (1973, 1975, 1976) and won 268 games against only 152 defeats. He won 20 or more games eight times, had an ERA of 2.86, and was elected to the Hall of Fame in 1990. The disagreements he had with his manager, Earl Weaver, were legendary. They usually centered around whether Palmer's various ailments were psychosomatic or not. Weaver once remarked, "I have more fights with Jim Palmer than with my wife."

IN LIGHT OF THEIR TEMPESTUOUS RELATIONSHIP, I ASKED THE WINNINGEST PITCHER OF THE 1970s IF HE AND EARL EVER SHARED A LIGHT MOMENT TOGETHER.

October 25, 1998

Dear Seth,

A moment I am fond of happened in the mid seventies in a game I pitched against the Texas Rangers. I had a 102° temperature and there was some question whether I would be able to pitch. I did and after retiring the Rangers in order in the 1st inning, the Orioles scored 5 runs in the bottom of the first. I was setting next to Earl Weaver and he looked at me and remarked, "I know you don't feel well, but imagine how sick you would feel if you were home, in bed and we scored 5 runs in the 1st." We both laughed and for one of the few times, I had to agree with Earl.

Sincerely,

WHIT WYATT

Born 1907, Kensington, Georgia. Whit pitched for five teams from 1929 to 1945, winning 106 games. One of manager Leo Durocher's "boys," Whit posted a 22−10 record for the Brooklyn Dodgers in their pennant-winning 1941 season. **I ASKED HIM FOR HIS IMPRESSIONS OF HIS OLD BOSS, THE LEGENDARY LEO "THE LIP."**

May 5, 1998

Seth:

Thought Leo Durocher was a great manager. Umpires-- they really hated him. In general, he'd get kicked out once or twice a week. But, he was a real pitcher's friend, always let us pitch our way out of trouble we started.

Things were different before the war. We HAD to win-- if we did, our familys ate better. Simple as that. Yeah, we threw at hitters every now and again to let them no whos boss. But, that's just baseball.

Sincerely,

**Whitlow Wyatt
Pitcher**

Whit and Leo, #2, argue a call, 1941 World Series.

VIC RASCHI

Born 1919, West Springfield, Massachusetts. Died 1988, Groveland, New York. The "Springfield Rifle" compiled a 132–66 won-lost record during a career that lasted from 1946 to 1955, playing most prominently with the powerful New York Yankees. His .667 winning percentage is fifth all-time. Along with Allie Reynolds, Eddie Lopat, and later Whitey Ford, the Yankees won five straight championships from 1949 to 1953 under manager Casey Stengel.

Raschi was one of Stengel's favorites. In this letter, written presumably to a fan, Raschi sums up the qualities that made Casey the great manager he was. **P.S. WHILE PITCHING FOR THE CARDINALS LATE IN HIS CAREER, RASCHI GAVE UP HANK AARON'S FIRST-EVER HOME RUN ON APRIL 23, 1954.**

October 3, 1979

Casey Stengel was a very nice person and human being. He helped all of his players and treated them as humans.

He was the most knowledgeable manager that I knew. He was always ahead of everyone else in decision making.

great guy.

Best wishes,
Vic Raschi

Casey

TERRY
COLLINS

Born 1949,
Midland,
Michigan. Terry is
entering his fourth
year as manager
of the Anaheim
Angels. Before
that he was the
Houston Astros'
skipper from
1994 to 1995.
He consistently
has his teams at
the top of the
standings.

**I ASKED HIM
WHETHER A
PITCHER EVER
REFUSED TO GIVE
HIM THE BALL
WHEN HE CAME
TO THE MOUND
TO TAKE HIM OUT.**

12/4/97

Dear Seth,

Thanks for your letter. In reference to your questions, No! Never has a pitcher refused to give me the ball. Many have tried to talk their way into staying in the game and some have succeeded.

But when I make my decision to take them out it is over!

I don't think pitchers resent coming out of a game but many do not want or like to come out. Some can't wait to get out!

Thanks for writing.
all the best
Terry Collins

2000
GENE AUTRY WAY
P.O. BOX 2000
ANAHEIM, CA 92806
© ANAHEIM ANGELS

PHONE
714-940-2000

FAX
714-940-2001

MIKE KRUKOW

Born 1952, Long Beach, California. Mike was a 124-game winner in his fourteen-year career (1976–1989) spent mostly with the Chicago Cubs and San Francisco Giants. In 1986, he had his best year when he won 20 and lost 9.

I ASKED MIKE WHETHER VISITS TO THE MOUND BY PITCHING COACHES WERE EVER HELPFUL.

Dear Seth,

Thank you for your letter. I heard from a friend of mine, Leonard Koppett, that you are doing this book.

The story was that in 1986 I was pitching in Philadelphia at Veteran's stadium. There was about 55,000 people there on this uncomfortably hot Sunday day. It was the 7th inning with one out and let's just say I had not been pitching my best. Norm Sherry was the pitching coach and Roger Craig, the Giants manager, sent Norm out to have a little talk with me. When a manager sends out his pitching coach the message is clear: 'get the next guy or you're gone'.

Norm had this way of walking with his head cocked down, like he was looking for change or something. During practice he was a baseball magnet, because with his head down he would never see all baseballs coming straight at him.

So Norm comes out, head down, into the field, hops over 3rd base, and was walking the last 5 or 6 feet of the astroturf before the pitcher's mound. When he was about a foot away he tripped and fell into a complete belly slide landing face down at the base of my feet.

Looking up at me from the base of the mound he said, "Do you think anyone saw that?" He proceeded to dust himself off and hurriedly walked back to the dugout, head down of course! I couldn't stop laughing. Bob Brenley, my catcher was there too and the whole stadium was roaring.

Let me tell you that was the most productive meeting I EVER had on the mound in all my years in baseball. After Sherry left, I threw a double play ball and we were out of the inning! I pitched a great game after that.

With Best Wishes,

Mike Krukow
Mike Krukow

RICHARD NIXON

Born 1913, Yorba Linda, California. Died 1994, New York City. The thirty-seventh president of the United States, Nixon was a diehard baseball fan, fond of receiving world championship teams at the White House. He was once quoted as saying, "If I had my life to live all over again, I'd have ended up as a sportswriter." Fifteen presidents have thrown out Opening Day ceremonial first pitches since William Howard Taft first did so on April 10, 1910. Franklin Roosevelt threw out the most, with eight, while Jimmy Carter never threw one out. Nixon threw out two, and his wife, Pat, was the first first lady to throw out an Opening Day first pitch.

In this letter to Yankee president Dan Topping, written during his first term as vice president, Nixon, against his wishes, had to decline the ultimate invitation for a baseball fan.

WHEN NIXON LOST HIS BID FOR THE WHITE HOUSE TO JOHN KENNEDY IN 1960, HE WAS REPORTEDLY OFFERED THE JOB AS BASEBALL COMMISSIONER.

OFFICE OF THE VICE PRESIDENT

WASHINGTON

July 27, 1955

Dear Dan:

As an ardent baseball fan I am greatly tempted to accept your invitation to be present on your Hall of Fame Day at Yankee Stadium.

There is nothing I would like better than to be there to see, in the flesh, such all-time greats as Ty Cobb, Tris Speaker, Bill Terry, Connie Mack, Clark Griffith, George Sisler, Lefty Grove, Mickey Cochrane, Frankie Frisch, Paul Waner, Fred Clarke, Cy Young, Ed Walsh, Al Simmons, Jimmy Foxx, Bill Dickey, Charley Gehringer, Mel Ott and many others whom I have read about and followed in the sports pages. And when you promise to have on hand the latest additions to the Cooperstown Shrine -- Joe DiMaggio, "Home Run" Baker, Dazzy Vance, Ray Schalk, Gabby Hartnett and Ted Lyons, the temptation becomes almost overpowering.

But much as I would like to be with you, I must remain in Washington for votes which are scheduled in the Senate on what may be the last day of the session.

Many thanks for the invitation and perhaps you can find some way of conveying my best wishes to these Titans of the baseball world.

Sincerely,

Richard Nixon

Mr. Daniel R. Topping
New York Yankees
745 Fifth Avenue
New York 22, New York

PROFESSOR HINTON'S BASEBALL GUN

As a way to prevent pitchers from getting "sore arm," in 1897, Princeton mathematics professor Charles "Bull" Hinton invented a baseball gun—a mechanical pitching device that could change speeds and throw curves. Using gunpowder to propel the ball from a cannonlike muzzle, it scared batters to death and was quickly discarded. Professor Hinton's other passion was the development of his theory that the universe has four dimensions. He called it his Theory of Higher Space.

ANNE PITCHER
BROSNAN

Born Staunton,

Virginia. When Anne

Pitcher married

hurler Jim Brosnan

(1954,

1956–1963,

Chicago Cubs,

Cincinnati Reds,

and two other

teams) it was pre-

sumably the only

time a Pitcher ever

married a pitcher.

I ASKED HER WHAT

BEING THE WIFE OF

A BIG-LEAGUE

PITCHER WAS LIKE.

April 18 1998

Seth,

In regards to your question about a Pitcher marrying a
Pitcher........Yes everyone that we knew though it was funny
that a Pitcher was marrying a Pitcher and amazingly enough
after all of these many years it still comes up once in
awhile and the person that says it thinks it has never been
said before.

What was it like for a wife of a big league pitcher
when her husband lost a big game?   Just a bad day at th e
office would be putting it mildly. In baseball or any oth e r
professional sport your office is there for everyone to see.
A relief pitcher and I might add his wife, can be subjected
to cheers or jeers depending on where one pitch goes when
you go into a ball game in late relief with the bases loaded,
no one out, and the winning run for the opposition at t he
plate. I asked Jim once if it bothered him if the fans booed
him when he lost and he said "No you don't hear or see the
fans." That did not turn out to be true in Cincinnati
when he went into a game with the bases loaded, no one out
and the wnning run at the plate and he went 3-2 on the batter.
I got so nervous that I got up from my seat and wen t to the
back of the stadium until he got out of the inning. Later
he said to me, "Why did you get up and leave? I had him
all the way." .....RIGHT !

I think most wives know when to stay away from their hus bands
when he loses a game. A martini, straught up, with an olive
usually took care of the situation.

It was a good ride

Sincerely,

Anne Pitcher Brosnan

The Brosnan Family, 1961.

BILL LEE

Born 1946, Burbank, California. "Spaceman" won 119 games with a 3.62 ERA, primarily for the Boston Red Sox and Montreal Expos during a career that spanned fourteen years (1969–1982). He will always be remembered for a big, slow curveball he threw to Tony Perez during the seventh game of the 1975 World Series. With two outs and one on in the sixth inning, and the Red Sox ahead 3–0, Perez hammered Lee's ill-advised offering, vaulting the "Big Red Machine" back into the contest, which they later won. Lee later commented, "I lived by the slow curve all year and I died by the slow curve." **I ASKED LEE WHY HE THREW THE PITCH. APPARENTLY, HE MUST HAVE THOUGHT THERE WAS ONE OUT AND SO WAS PERTURBED THAT DON ZIMMER DID NOT POSITION SECOND BASEMAN DENNY DOYLE AT DOUBLE-PLAY DEPTH.**

New England Grey Socks

Player/General Manager
WILLIAM FRANCIS LEE III

Seth.

as you can see my Knee hard Socks if you want the Rool story. one thing I remember Before Perez. Zimmer moved Doyle out ot Double Play Position!

Check out Full replay of Game.

Bill.

MULROONEY ON THE HILL

One night I decided to write a poem based on a fictional pitcher named Mulrooney. When the poem was completed, I found out Minnesota Twins pitcher Bob Tewksbury was also an accomplished illustrator, so I asked him if he would be interested in doing some illustrations for the poem. I was thrilled when he agreed.

"Tewks" was born in 1960 in Concord, New Hampshire. He broke in with the Yankees in 1986, has pitched for the Cubs, Cardinals, and Twins, compiling a record of 110–102. He is known for his great control, surrendering only 1.29 every nine innings, best among pitchers in the 90s. His best year was 1992, when he won 16–5, with a 2.16 ERA pitching for St. Louis. He announced his retirement in 1999.

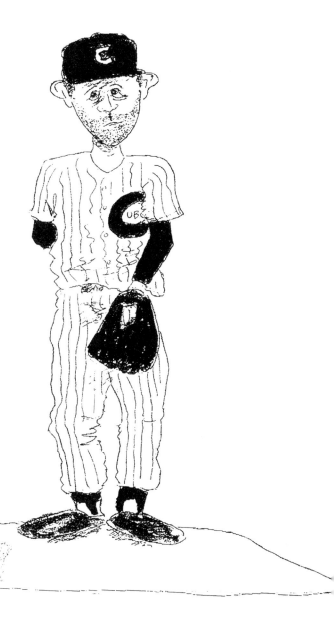

Mulrooney On The Hill
by Seth Swirsky

Two outs and bases loaded
In the final Series game,
The Cubs were but a strike away
From popping the champagne.

The breathing of the multitudes
Was for one minute still,
As they all stared at the starter,
Mulrooney on the hill.

The catcher called for a breaking ball
That pitch would surely do it.
Mulrooney went into his stretch,
Then twisted back and threw it.

"Ball one" the grumpy ump barked out,
As if the crowd was hard of hearing,
But all was deadly quiet,
The denouement was nearing.

The catcher thrust three fingers down
Now calling for the slider,
And it surely would have been strike three,
Had the plate been four feet wider!

"Ball two" then boomed the man in black,
From close behind the plate,
Still, one more strike would do the trick,
But the fans would have to wait.

For quickly to the mound now stalked
The manager to see,
If his ace still had the stuff,
To nail down strike three.

"You've had enough, kid," said the coach,
In a rolling southern drawl
But Mulrooney would not listen,
And would not give up the ball!

"I'll get him, boss," the hurler said,
"I swear, this time I will,"
So queasily, the skipper left,
Mulrooney on the hill.

Some vocal fans yelled from the stands,
"C'mon, Mulrooney, get 'em!"
But others kept things to themselves,
(For fear they would upset him.)

The next pitch was a spitter,
Which he threw with extra zing
And it almost fooled the hitter
But he held up on his swing.

And when the ump declared "ball three",
Then everybody knew
That the next pitch would decide the game;
The count was three and two.

A   dark cloud hovered overhead
Where once the sky was clear,
One more ball, and the Cubs would fall for
Yet another year.

The catcher ...rew two fingers down,
To signal for the curve,
But Mulrooney, poor Mulrooney,
Simply didn't have the nerve.

He knew then if he blew it
He would join a special circle
That included guys with names like Buckner,
Snodgrass, Moore and Merkle.

So,to himself, Mulrooney said,
"This ain't no time to fiddle.
I gotta' throw my finest pitch,
A fastball down the middle."

Shaking off his catcher's cue,
The pitcher blazed his heat.
The scene seemed in slow motion
As the crowd rose to its feet.

They watched the ball spin homeward
And hit the catcher's leather
But waiting for the umps last call-
Just seemed to take forever.

The ump looked at Mulrooney,
As the rain began to pour.
Then 50,000, heard his words,
Those dreadful words - "ball four."

And as the winning run touched home,
There came a crackling sound.
A silver bolt of lightening
Had struck the pitchers mound.

The baseball Gods were speaking,
To every Cub believer,
When in doubt, replace your ace,
With your best reliever.

Many years have passed since then
And yet the bitter pill
For Cub fans is the memory of
Mulrooney on the hill.

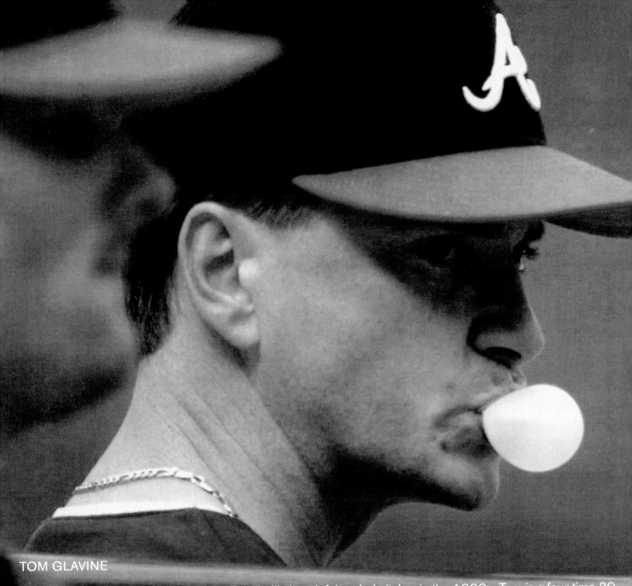

TOM GLAVINE

Born 1966, Concord, Massachusetts. Baseball's best left-handed pitcher in the 1990s, Tom is a four-time 20 game winner, having won 175 games pitching for the Atlanta Braves from 1987 to the present. Riding the nastiest change-up in the game, he won the Cy Young Award in 1991 and 1998, and was named the 1995 World Series Most Valuable Player. A likely future Hall of Famer, Glavine is among baseball's most well-liked and respected ballplayers. **WITH EVERYTHING HE HAS ALREADY ACHIEVED, I WONDERED WHAT MOTIVATES HIM TO CONTINUE TO SUCCEED.**

WORLD CHAMPIONS
1995
NATIONAL LEAGUE CHAMPIONS
1991 • 1992 • 1995 • 1996
DIVISION CHAMPIONS
1969 • 1982 • 1991 • 1992
1993 • 1995 • 1996 • 1997

Dear Seth,

Competition is what drives me—Competition between me myself and the hitter trying to be better than him. also, the Competition with myself trying to get better year in and year out and not Setteling for where I am and the success I've had— the Competition makes the game So much fun, and beleive me, it really is a great way to make a living!

Sincerely

Tom Glavine

DICKIE KERR

Born 1893, St. Louis, Missouri. Died 1963, Houston,
Texas. A five-foot-seven lefty, Dickie pitched for the
Chicago White Sox from 1919 to 1921 and in 1925,
compiling an impressive 53–24 won-lost record. Unlike
many of his teammates on the infamous 1919 "Black
Sox," who conspired to throw the World Series, Kerr
didn't take the bribe money offered to many of his better-
salaried teammates. He started and won two games in
that tainted Series. In 1922, he appeared in a semipro
game with many of his blacklisted ex-teammates. For that
action, he was banished from the majors by
Commissioner Kenesaw Mountain Landis. The ban was
lifted in 1925, but by then Kerr's effectiveness as a
pitcher was gone. Knowing only baseball, he
knocked around the game, in various capacities for
the rest of his life.

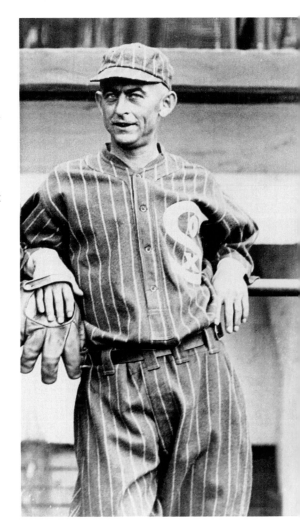

Kerr's letter, written presumably to someone
affiliated with a minor league ball club, shows how hard
work was to come by, for even the most honest and
experienced of men, in Depression-era America.

Stan Musial named his first son after Kerr in grati-
tude for Kerr's advice, early in Stan's career, to quit
pitching and convert to the outfield. Musial became one
of the game's great hitters. When Dickie fell on hard
times, Musial bought him a home in Houston.

BLYTHEVILLE, ARKANSAS Sept -11-1938.

Friend

I am trying to line up a job for 1939 in base ball.

Do not care what kind, whether as manager, coach or scout, so am writing you to find out if you can place me some where.

See where Hot Springs will be your farm next year, would like to go there and develop some ball players for you.

May I hear from you soon?

With kindest regards, I am

Dick Kerr

124 E. CHERRY-ST.

1920s, a Pennsylvania man named William Bennethum was a pitcher on the local Reading

...ub, which played against some of the barnstorming teams that passed through town. The barn-

...ere made up mostly of major leaguers looking for extra money to supplement their small base-

...s. Bennethum pitched against some of the all-time greats and also heard stories from them

...vorite players, especially "Shoeless Joe" Jackson. The disgraced Jackson, one of the greatest

...aseball history, had been banned from the game in 1920 for being one of eight players to

...ney to throw the 1919 World Series. Bennethum still thought Joe was the greatest hitter he had

...He recounted all the baseball tales he knew for his two sons every night as they lay in bed. One

...Bill Junior, was so taken with his father's vivid recollections of "Shoeless Joe" that he wrote a

letter to him (opposite page) requesting his autograph.

Joe had never learned to read or write. His wife Katie signed all of her husband's autograph requests, and that's what Bill got back in the mail. When Joe died, Joe's sister found among his personal effects the original letter young Bill had written to him, tucked inside its original envelope. Joe had kept it. On the back of the envelope, Joe practiced signing his name for the boy. Joe, ashamed of his illiteracy, never sent it.

Dear Mr. Jackson

I am in 8th Grade and am 13 yrs. old My father talks about you very much. He considers you the best ballplayer ever lived second only to the great Ty Cobb. I play left field on my school team. My hobby is baseball. I read about you in books. Will you please send me your autograph. I have enclosed an envelope with my name and address on it and a piece of paper for you to sign on. Thank you very much.

Sincerely yours,
William Bennethum
432 north 10th St.
Reading, Pennsylvania

JUDGE KENESAW MOUNTAIN LANDIS

Born November 1866, Millville, Ohio. Died November 25, 1944, Chicago, Illinois. Judge Landis was elected the first commissioner of baseball on November 12, 1920. On the heels of tardy revelations of the 1919
Black Sox scandal and other gambling-related improprieties, baseball was in dire need of credibility. Although
the Black Sox Eight were acquitted on August 2, 1921, by a jury verdict, Landis banned all eight from playing in the majors again based on leaked testimony that proved the conspiracy. Landis was a near fanatic when
it came to the mixing of baseball and gambling. His conviction is evident in his response (opposite page) to
Joe Jackson's request for reinstatement to the game. To this day the controversy simmers, as Jackson is still
not eligible for the Hall of Fame. Landis served as commissioner until his death.

BASEBALL

KENESAW M. LANDIS
COMMISSIONER
LESLIE M. O'CONNOR
SECRETARY-TREASURER

122 SOUTH MICHIGAN AVENUE
CHICAGO
July 16, 1923.

Mr. Joe Jackson,
Bastrop, La.

Dear Sir:

Your letter, which is dated 7-29, came here in
my absence and through an error in forwarding, was delayed
in coming to my attention.

Before I can pass upon your application for
reinstatement, it will be necessary for you to forward to
me for consideration in that connection, a full statement
in detail of your conduct and connection with the arrange-
ment for the "throwing" of the World's Series of 1919. I
feel I should say to you that there will be no reinstatement
of any player who had any connection therewith.

Very truly yours,

KML:B

75

Pete Rose, 1963

BOB FRIEND

Born 1930, Lafayette, Indiana. A durable and effective starting pitcher, he spent most of his fifteen-year career (1951–1966) with the Pittsburgh Pirates. On April 13, 1963, Bob gave up a triple to a rookie named Pete Rose. It was "Charlie Hustle's" first hit in the major leagues. He would have 4,255 more over the span of his amazing twenty-four-year career, eventually becoming baseball's all-time hits leader. In 1989, Commissioner Bart Giamatti banned Rose from baseball for betting on the game, and at present he is not eligible for induction into the Hall of Fame. **I ASKED FRIEND WHAT HE REMEMBERED ABOUT HIS FIRST ENCOUNTER WITH BASEBALL'S EVENTUAL ALL-TIME HIT KING.**

BABB, INC.

INSURANCE BROKERS SINCE 1929

The Winning Team in Health Care Plan Administration

April 1, 1997

Mr. Seth Swirsky
November Nights Music Inc.

Dear Seth:

Thanks for your letter. It's nice to hear from baseball enthusiasts. I do remember my first encounter with Pete Rose.

It was a bright, suuny April day in Cincinnati at Crosley Field, home of the cincinnati Reds. Since Pete was one of the most talked about rookies that spring, most of us knew about his previous heroics and his ability to turn a game around. I remember Pete that day as a very aggressive hitter at the plate. He stood close to the plate, fouled many pitches off until he got the one he wanted. My recollection it was a fast ball on the right corner of the plate and he tripled down the left field line. *Of course, with his great speed, he didn't even have to slide going into third base.*

Noone knew at the time the significance of that first hit to Pete. He is a true Hall of Famer. Hope some day he will make it to Cooperstown.

Thanks again for your interest.

Sincerely,

Robert B. Friend

FAY VINCENT

Born 1938, Waterbury, Connecticut. He became the commissioner of baseball in September 1989, upon the death of his predecessor and good friend, Bart Giamatti. Vincent's term lasted two years. Opposition by the owners to his plans for realignment were among the many issues that led to his dismissal in 1991.

I ASKED HIM WHO WERE THE BEST PITCHERS HE SAW GROWING UP AND WHILE HE WAS COMMISSIONER.

Francis T. Vincent, Jr.

May 19, 1998

Dear Seth:

Thanks for writing me. I'm interested you were born in New Haven. I lived there (on Orange Street) as a kid and one of the loves Bart Giamatti and I shared was for New Haven, Wooster Street and Pepe's Pizza. You, too?

The best pitcher I ever saw in person was Bob Gibson, though as a kid I loved Allie Reynolds and Whitey Ford. Gibson's fastball in the 60's was over powering; a much over used word but I saw him one-hit the Mets with only a bloop single by Ron Hunt spoiling it. His physical presence was part of his intimidation and I doubt anyone will have a better year than his best in those 60's.

My best day watching pitchers was an evening I spent with Eddie Lopat at Yankee Stadium while I was Commissioner. He was so smart that it was a full education to have him comment on each pitch and tell me why the pitchers today don't think as well as they should. Bobby Brown says Lopat was the smartest pitcher he ever saw and I agree. Remember Casey said Lopat "threw tissue paper".

Best,

Fay Vincent

Fay Vincent

11/28/97

Seth,

. I'd say the biggest difference ~~when~~ watching baseball in the late 1990's compared to playing in the late 60's and early 70's was the depth of quality starting pitching. In the National League, almost every team had ~~at~~ least two quality starters and ~~they~~ many had three or four. There weren't too many soft touches. They also went deeper into the game so one didn't get to face a lot of the watered down mid-relief pitching so prevalent today.

Guys like Curt Shilling and Roger Clemens are throw-backs to another era. Power, power and more power. I'd compare Shilling to Denny McLain's years of 1968 and 1969 and Clemens to Tom Seaver. Luis Tiant in his prime would compare favorably to Pedro Martinez but it's tough to compare Greg Maddux to anyone from that era as he's so unique. Pedro also would compare to Bob Gibson because they both had a mean streak.

It's also ~~much~~ tougher to pitch today because of a much smaller strike zone, especially in the American League.

Good Luck

Dave Campbell

DAVE CAMPBELL

Born 1942, Manistee, Michigan. Dave was a utility player for four teams from 1967 to 1974, including the world champion 1968 Detroit Tigers. He's considered one of the more insightful television baseball analysts in the game. Currently, he is the color commentator for the Colorado Rockies and can also be seen on ESPN's *Baseball Tonight.* **I ASKED HIM WHAT IS THE BIGGEST DIFFERENCE BETWEEN PLAYING BASEBALL IN THE 1960s AND WATCHING BASEBALL IN THE 1990s.**

LUIS TIANT

Born 1940, Marianao, Cuba. "El Tiante" won 229 games with a 3.30 ERA during a colorful career (1964–1982) most memorably spent with the Boston Red Sox and Cleveland Indians. With his legendary twists and turns, he brought the ball homeward with a unique variety of styles that threw hitters off balance. A dominant competitor during his long career, he deserves serious Hall of Fame consideration.

I ASKED HIM WHAT MOMENT HE SAVORS MOST FROM HIS CAREER AND HOW HE DEVELOPED HIS UNFORGET-TABLE PITCHING MOTION.

DEAR SETH

MY MOST SATISFYING MOMENT IN BASEBALL WAS MY 1ST GAME IN THE BIG LEAGER AGAINS THE YANKEES,

I WON 3-0 AND STRUCKOUT 11. ALSO TIED A RECORD BY STRIKING OUT 11 IN MY 1ST M.L START.

I GOT MY ORIGINAR DELIVERY BY SHOWING MY NUMBER TO THE BATTER.

I STARTED THIS IN BOSTON. I THEN STARTED TO LOOK AT THE CLOUDS AND THE PEOPLE. AND SINCE IT WORK I KEPT DOING IT.

[signature]

PEDRO MARTINEZ

Born 1971, Manoguayabo, Dominican Republic. When the Boston Red Sox lost fan favorite, future Hall-of-Famer Roger Clemens to free agency in 1997 to the Toronto Blue Jays, the Boston general manager Dan Duquette went out and got the 1997 National League Cy Young winner, Pedro Martinez. The competitively intense Martinez started his career with the Los Angeles Dodgers (1992–1993), played for the Montreal Expos in 1994–1997, before being picked up by the Red Sox for the highest salary in baseball history at the time. In his first year with the Sox (1998), he won 19 with 251 strikeouts. His career won-lost record is 84–46, a .646 winning percentage ranking him fourth among active pitchers. In the 1990s, Pedro held opposing batters to a .214 batting average, second only to Randy Johnson. With 1,221 career strikeouts in 1,146 innings, he ranks near or at the top of "Who's the best pitcher in the game today?" lists.

I ASKED PEDRO WHETHER IT WAS HARDER TO PITCH IN BOSTON THAN IN MONTREAL OR LOS ANGELES.

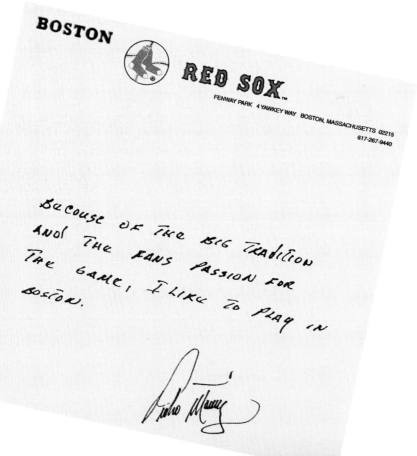

BOSTON RED SOX

FENWAY PARK 4 YAWKEY WAY BOSTON, MASSACHUSETTS 02215
617-267-9440

Because of the big tradition and the fans passion for the game, I like to play in Boston.

CHET HOFF

Born 1891, Ossining, New York. Died 1998, Daytona Beach, Florida. "Red," as he was known, was the oldest living baseball player of all time at 107½ years old. A five-foot-nine lefty, he pitched for the New York Highlanders (before they were the Yankees) from 1911 to 1913 and the St. Louis Browns in 1915, finishing his career with a record of 2 wins, 4 losses, and an ERA of 2.49. **I ASKED HIM IF HE REMEMBERED THE FIRST BATTER HE FACED EIGHTY-SEVEN YEARS EARLIER. (HIS RESPONSE WAS DICTATED TO AN ATTENDANT AT THE NURSING HOME WHERE HE RESIDED. CHET THEN SIGNED IT.)**

I hoped for a great game.
It was the 1st game I ever played with the Yankees and surprisingly enough I ended up pitching to Ty Cobb. I remember striking out Ty Cobb that day — He was the only batter that I ever had 400. a great guy —

Chet Hoff

This is what a game of baseball looked like at Hilltop Park when Chet faced Cobb. He didn't even know it was Cobb he struck out until he read it in the newspaper the next day.

JARET WRIGHT

Born 1975, Anaheim, California. A Cleveland Indian fastballer (1997–present), Jaret was the youngest pitcher ever to start a seventh game of a World Series when he faced the Florida Marlins, at age twenty-one, in Game Seven of the 1997 Fall Classic. He pitched brilliantly, giving up just two runs and maintaining the lead until the Indians' bullpen lost the game in the ninth. **I WONDERED IF HIS DAD, FORMER MAJOR-LEAGUE PITCHER CLYDE WRIGHT, SAID ANYTHING TO HIM BEFORE AND AFTER THE BIG GAME.**

I HAD SPOKE TO MY DAD JUST A LITTLE BEFORE THE GAME AND HE SAID TO ENJOY WHAT WAS GOING ON AND TO HAVE CONFIDENCE IN MYSELF. AFTER THE GAME HE SAID THAT I SHOULD BE PROUD OF WHAT THE TEAM AND MYSELF HAD DONE.

CLYDE WRIGHT

Born 1941, Jefferson City, Tennessee. Clyde won 100 games during his ten-year career, spent mostly with the California Angels (1966–1975). His best season was in 1970, when he won 22 and lost 12 with a 2.83 earned run average. **I ASKED HIM IF IT WAS HARD WATCHING HIS SON JARET START THE SEVENTH GAME OF THE 1997 WORLD SERIES AGAINST THE FLORIDA MARLINS.**

Nov 28, 1998

Seth,

Yes, it was hard to watch my son pitch the seventh game. It was twice as hard for my wife to watch! Every parent wants their kids to do well. It doesn't matter what field.

Jaret just happened to be on National T.V. with millions of people watching. The one thing that calmed me down was Big Jack Nicklaus was there. I kept telling myself "he came to see my son pitch!" Yes, I know he is from Florida, Wishful Thinking!

Clyde Wright

By the time Jaret was a Junior in H.S, I knew he had a good chance to play pro-ball,

HUB KITTLE

Born 1917, Los Angeles, California. A longtime Cardinal minor-league pitcher and coach, Hub is the oldest person in history ever to play in an organized baseball game. On August 27, 1980, at the age of 63½, he started an American Association game and pitched one and a third innings, not giving up a hit. Having pitched in organized baseball in every decade since the 1930s, his appearance that night made Hub the only man ever to play in six different decades. **I ASKED HIM HOW HIS AMAZING PITCHING APPEARANCE CAME ABOUT.**

EAT AT
HUB KITTLE'S
Specializing Chili
Steaks Short Orders
WE NEVER CLOSE
Ph. 3926
28½ S. 2nd St.

July 21, 1998

Dear Seth:

Some think Satchel Paige or Lefty O'Doul were the oldest to play in a professional, organized baseball game but no, it was me, ol' Hub.

One day, A. Ray Smith, the owner of the Springfield team ,where I was a pitching coach, asked me if I would pitch as a promotion. "Sure" I says, not really taking him that seriously. I was 63 and a half years old at the time!

A few weeks later, I was up in the press box and all the reporters up there they says "Hey Hub, did you know you're going to start tomorrow night?" I said "What!?" I walked in the office and Alice, the owners secretary handed me a contract to sign for $1.00. So I signed it. The next night we had the game against a triple A team Des Moines. I warmed up in the bullpen, felt pretty good.

Before I knew it, I'm on the mound in front of a packed house. When I took my hat off for the National Anthem, my bald spot was shining in the moonlight. Jody Davis was my catcher, soon to play for the Cubs.

I looked down at the first batter and I swear to God he looked like he was two miles away. He looked so small. I was used to throwing B.P.(batting practice) up in front of the rubber all the time and now I had to throw it what seemed like a mile. So I says to myself 'what are you doing here you dumb, dumb, dumb donkey?'

I took my wind-up on the first hitter and I'll be damned if he didn't try to bunt the ball off of me. The ball went foul and I said to him as he went by: 'with the next pitch, you are going down on your gazaba boy!' Next pitch I put right under his chin. All the fans clapped like hell. I got him out and got the next two batters plus the first hitter in the next inning and that was that.

The oldest man ever to play in a baseball game,

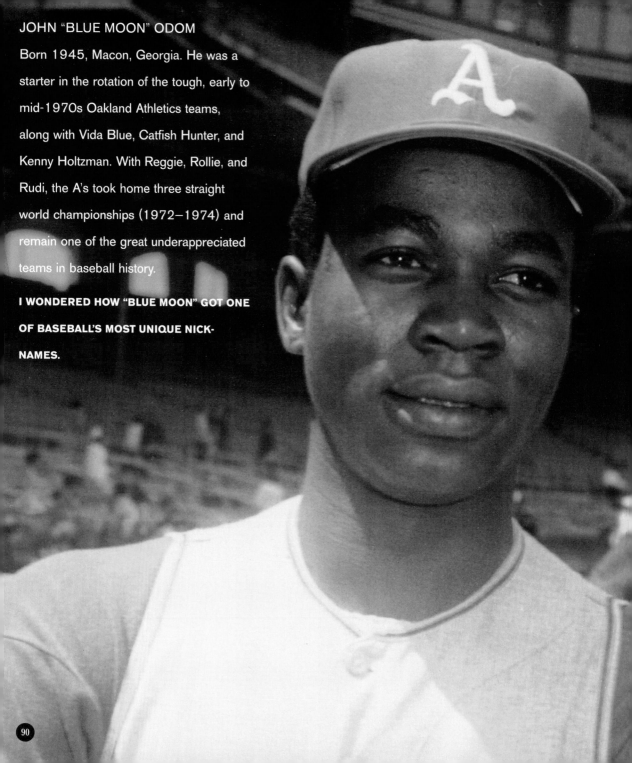

JOHN "BLUE MOON" ODOM

Born 1945, Macon, Georgia. He was a starter in the rotation of the tough, early to mid-1970s Oakland Athletics teams, along with Vida Blue, Catfish Hunter, and Kenny Holtzman. With Reggie, Rollie, and Rudi, the A's took home three straight world championships (1972–1974) and remain one of the great underappreciated teams in baseball history.

I WONDERED HOW "BLUE MOON" GOT ONE OF BASEBALL'S MOST UNIQUE NICK-NAMES.

Dear Seth

My Nickname "Blue moon" was given to me in the fifth grade, by a classmate by the name of Joe Morris. It frist started out by him using the name "Moon Head" and shortly after went to "Blue moon".

Ever since that has been my nickname. alot of people believe that Charles O. Finley the former Oakland A's owner gave me the "Nickname". He did Name a few of the players such as "Catfish"

In the beginery; I did not like it; after a while I got used to it and ever since it has stuck!

John "Blue moon" Odom
Oakland A's #13

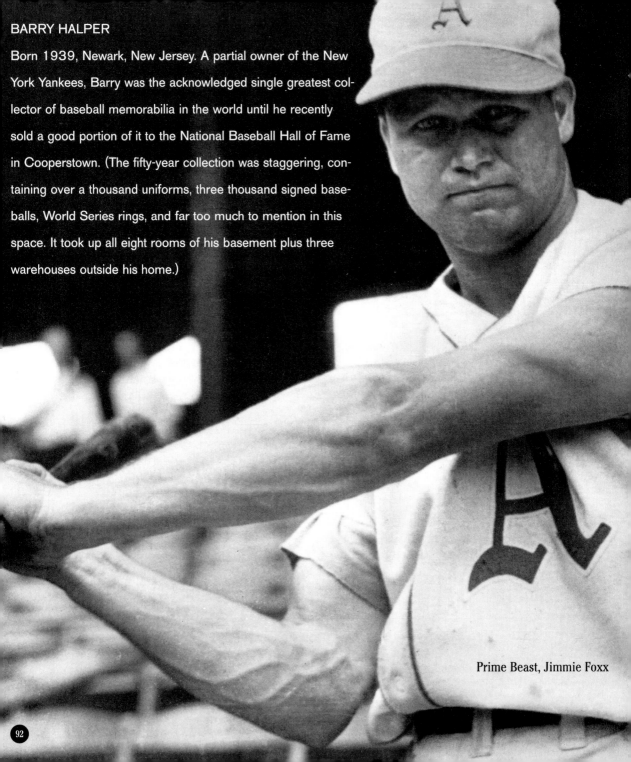

BARRY HALPER

Born 1939, Newark, New Jersey. A partial owner of the New York Yankees, Barry was the acknowledged single greatest collector of baseball memorabilia in the world until he recently sold a good portion of it to the National Baseball Hall of Fame in Cooperstown. (The fifty-year collection was staggering, containing over a thousand uniforms, three thousand signed baseballs, World Series rings, and far too much to mention in this space. It took up all eight rooms of his basement plus three warehouses outside his home.)

Prime Beast, Jimmie Foxx

In the late 1950s, Barry pitched for the University of Miami, where his baseball coach was one of the game's great sluggers, "Double X," Jimmie Foxx. Foxx, from Sudlersville, Maryland (born 1907), hit 534 career home runs, second only to Babe Ruth during his day. Foxx also had a .325 batting average, won two MVPs in 1932 and 1933 and the Triple Crown in 1933. "The Beast," as Foxx was also known, played most notably for the Philadelphia A's (1925–1935) and the Boston Red Sox (1936–1942) before retiring in 1945. Foxx choked to death in Miami in 1967, while dining with his brother.

I ASKED BARRY IF HE EVER HAD A CHANCE TO PITCH AGAINST HIS COACH, THE DEVASTATING JIMMIE FOXX.

October 13, 1997

Dear Seth:

With reference to your letter of September 26th, I will attempt to give you visual description of what it was like to pitch to the Double X.

In 1957 I was a freshman at the University of Miami and a walk-on during the baseball workouts. I was a pitcher in high school and specifically wanted to go to Miami's warm weather to possibly play ball all year around. There were other walk-ons also but I was the only pitcher so our coach at the University of Miami, Jimmie Foxx, said okay Halper, warm up, you go in next (we had a scrimmage game).

I threw about twenty pitches on the side line and announced that I was ready. Jimmie said, I'm glad you mentioned you were ready but why didn't you throw any fast balls!! When I told him they were my fast balls he chuckled and said, okay, go on out there and throw strikes. In those days, there were no jugs to determine how fast your pitch was so you had to go by sight and sound. I'm sure that I did not break 80 but what I did have was an excellent curve ball, thrown in three different styles - side arm, 3/4 and completely overhead, which is where the term "drop ball" came about in my era.

After striking out the first two batters in sweeping curve balls, Foxx came out of the dug out, swinging two bats in his right hand as if he was getting ready to go to home plate to hit. He chased the next scheduled batter out of the cage and told him to do ten laps and then he could hit. He went to the box and looked down at me at the mound. Now, don't forget - I was trying to make this team at 18 years old and here is a Hall of Famer in the batters box!!!

He chirped from the box - I want you to throw me those rinky dink curve balls you threw to the others but if you hit me, you're gonna run from today until tomorrow. I took my wind-up, aimed right at the batters left elbow and said to myself, please God, let it go over the plate (which it did). Throw me another and don't hit me, he screamed. The second pitch went the same way, right over the plate. He said Okay, I think I have it gauged now, one more. I threw the third pitch, the same as the others, except this time he swung and hit a monstrous fly ball which disappeared over the left field wall and with it, I thought, my dreams of playing at University of Miami. My reward for being such a good pupil was at first, ten laps around the track but when I answered him I said, you said don't hit me and I didn't hit you. He said, yes, but you let an old man go deep, now its up to twenty laps!!! (Don't forget, after all, the man was fifty years old at the time!!) That's exactly how it happened.

I never did get to speak to Jimmie Foxx about the toughest pitcher he ever faced but he was true to his nickname, The Beast. He used to be proud that that's what they called him and probably a name that a lot of people don't know about. Babe Ruth, who never remembered anybody's name, gave him the nickname The Beast and the way Coach Foxx explained it, Babe told him he was the "Fu---n' Beast"!!! He has a massive upper body with the arms of a lumberjack.

Thank you for your kind words about my collection and I look forward to your next book.

One last comment -- the greatest pitcher ever? I would say although I never saw him pitch, it would have to be Mathewson. Look up what he did in the 1905 World Series, pitching three shut outs within a space of five days. If that was today, he probably would have only gotten to pitch one game, the way they molly-coddle today's players.

With kindest personal regards,

BARRY HALPER

CHRISTY MATHEWSON

Born 1880, Factoryville, Pennsylvania. Died 1925, Saranac Lake, New York. Mathewson, who pitched from 1900 to 1916, is tied with Grover Cleveland Alexander as the winningest pitcher in National League history with 373 victories (third all-time). He had a .665 winning percentage (seventh all-time) and a 2.13 ERA (fifth all-time). In World Series play, he started 11 games (second all-time) and completed 10 (first all-time).

In the 1905 World Series, he shut out the Philadelphia A's three times in the course of five afternoons.

While working in a chemical lab in France during World War I, Christy was exposed to poisonous gas that severely damaged his lungs. In 1925, at the age of 45, he contracted and died of tuberculosis, a direct result of his exposure to chemicals.

THESE ARE MATHEWSON'S ORDERS TO REPORT FOR THE GREAT WAR THAT ULTIMATELY TOOK HIS LIFE, SEVEN YEARS AFTER WAR'S END.

HEADQUARTERS PORT OF EMBARKATION
HOBOKEN, NEW JERSEY

September 11th, 1918

CONFIDENTIAL.

From: Adjutant.

To: Captain Christopher Mathewson, C. W. S., (Item E 921 K)

Subject: Travel Orders.

1. Having reported at these Headquarters, this date, in compliance with War Department orders dated   September 6th, 1918. 1917, you will report, without delay, to the General Superintendent of Army Transport Service, Hoboken, New Jersey, for transportation abroad. to France,

2. Upon arriving at your destination, you will report to The Commanding General, American Expeditionary Forces, for assignment to duty under the Chief of Chemical Warfare Service.

3. The travel directed is necessary in the military service.

By command of Major General Shanks:

D. A. Watt

Adjutant General.

s/d

TRANSPORTATION FURNISHED ON THIS ORDER
FROM NEW YORK CITY TO LIVERPOOL, ENG.
A. C. DALTON,
GEN'L SUPT U. S. A. T. S.
BY J. C. HUTCHESON
1ST LIEUT. Q.M.C

WALTER JOHNSON

Born 1887, Humboldt, Kansas. Died 1946, Washington, D.C. Considered by many experts to be the greatest pitcher ever, "The Big Train" won 417 games pitching for the hitting-poor Washington Senators. He pitched 110 shutouts and went 36–7, with a 1.09 ERA in 1913. The 5,924 innings he pitched are third most all-time.

His humble disposition and incomparable fastball made him one of the game's most respected players. On August 2, 1927, the twentieth anniversary of the first game Walter pitched for

WALTER JOHNSON
WASHINGTON, D. C.

1927

I Saw
Walter
Pitch the
First Game

August 3, 1927

1907

Dear Friend:

As one of those who saw me pitch my first game in Washington, I am grateful to you for your attendance at the Twentieth Anniversary game on August 2, 1927, and for your fine support throughout the intervening years. I very much appreciate the way in which you and other baseball patrons here in Washington and elsewhere have shown their regard for me and I regret it was not possible to greet you personally at the game.

Sincerely yours,

Walter Johnson

them, the Senators had a "Walter Johnson Day" at Griffith Park. Walter's true appreciation of the fans is evident in this letter he wrote to an admirer he was unable to greet that festive afternoon. In the upper right corner is the silk that Walter kept for himself as a souvenir of the game in which he was honored.

sons as a starter, he won 223 games with 186 losses and a 3.80 earned run average. Between 1932 and 1939, he averaged seventeen victories a year, winning twenty games twice. In the 1934 All-Star game, in which National League strikeout king Carl Hubbell struck out Ruth, Gehrig, Foxx, Simmons, and Cronin consecutively, Harder pitched five innings of one-hit relief ball to get the win for the American League. He also saved the 1935 and 1937 All-Star games. In 1990, the Indians retired his #18, one of only five players to be so honored by the Tribe.

FROM 1933 TO 1935, THE LEGENDARY WALTER JOHNSON MANAGED THE INDIANS. I ASKED HARDER HIS RECOL-LECTIONS OF THE GREAT HURLER.

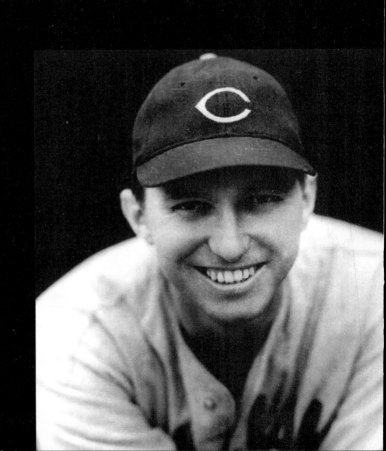

9/16/97

Dear Seth:

I pitched for Walter Johnson
in 1933, 34 and 35 and they were the best
years of my career.

Walter was a High Class, Gentleman
type person and easy Man to work for.

Muddy Ruel, who caught Walter
at Washington and later a Coach for
Cleveland tells how Walter, who had the
best Fast ball in Baseball, would shake-off
'Muddy's' fast ball sign, so he could throw
his little curve ball. Walter was proud of
his curve, but 'Muddy' would always make
him to throw his fast balls-

I believe Walter Johnson was the
greatest Pitcher of all time.

Best Regards,

Mel Harder

BILL WAMBSGANSS

Born 1894, Cleveland, Ohio. Died 1985, Lakewood, Ohio. "Wamby" was a utility infielder during his thirteen-year career (1914–1926) spent with the Cleveland Indians, Boston Red Sox and Philadelphia Athletics. He will forever be remembered for two things: his offbeat, hard-to-pronounce surname and the unassisted triple play he pulled off during the 1920 World Series as a member of the Cleveland Indians. It remains the only triple play in World Series history. **WAMBSGANSS RECALLS THE BEST PITCHER HE FACED DURING HIS YEARS IN BASEBALL.**

Wambsganss in the midst of his World Series triple play

The greatest pitcher that I ever saw and batted against was Walter Johnson.

The greatest hitter was Babe Ruth. There was also Ty Cobb. Ruth also was a very good lefthanded pitcher I batted against him too

Hamley

Born 1900, Lonaconing, Maryland. Died 1975, Norwalk, Ohio. Considered by many the greatest left-hander of all time, Robert Moses "Lefty" Grove was a temperamental man who pitched for the Philadelphia Athletics (1925–1933) and the Boston Red Sox (1934–1941). He compiled a record of 300–141 (a .680 winning percentage, fourth all-time), and won 20 games or more eight out of the nine years between 1927 and 1935. He was elected to the Hall of Fame in 1947.

In 1931, he had his greatest season, winning 31 and losing just 4 with a 2.06 ERA (he led his league in ERA a major-league-record nine times). He retired on December 7, 1941, the day Pearl Harbor was bombed, and opened up a bowling alley in his hometown.

On the following page is Lefty's 1931 player's contract.

IMPORTANT NOTICE

The attention of both **Club** and **Player** is specifically directed to the following excerpt from **Article II, Section 1,** of the **Major League Rules:**

"No Club shall make a contract different from the uniform contract or a contract containing a non-reserve clause, except with the written approval of the Advisory Council. All contracts shall be in duplicate and the Player shall retain a counterpart original. The making of any agreement between a Club and Player not embodied in the contract shall subject both parties to discipline by the Commissioner."

American League of Professional Baseball Clubs
UNIFORM PLAYER'S CONTRACT

Parties   The ....,

herein called the Club, and.....Robert M. Grove...,

           89 Douglass Avenue,

of ....Lonaconing, Md.........................., herein called the Player.

Recital   The club is a member of the American League of Professional Baseball Clubs. As such, and jointly with the other members of the League, it is a party to agreements and rules with the National League of Professional Baseball Clubs and its constituent clubs, and with the National Association of Professional Baseball Leagues. The purpose of these agreements and rules is to insure to the public wholesome and high-class professional baseball by defining the relations between Club and Player, between club and club, between league and league, and by vesting in a designated Commissioner broad powers of control and discipline, and of decision in case of disputes.

Agreement   In view of the facts above recited the parties agree as follows:

Employment   1. The Club hereby employs the Player to render skilled service as a baseball player in connection

with all games of the Club during the year.. 193..1.............................. including the Club's training season, the Club's exhibition games, the Club's playing season, and the World Series (or any other official series in which the Club may participate and in any receipts of which the player may be entitled to share); and the player covenants that he will perform with diligence and fidelity the service stated and such duties as may be required of him in such employment.

Salary   2. For the service aforesaid the Club will pay the Player an aggregate salary of $20,000 no.

............................, as follows:

In semi-monthly installments after the commencement of the playing season covered by this contract, unless the Player is "abroad" with the Club for the purpose of playing games, in which event the amount then due shall be paid on the first week-day after the return "home" of the Club, the terms *"home"* and *"abroad"* meaning, respectively, *at* and *away from* the city in which the Club has its baseball field.

If a monthly salary is stipulated above, it shall begin with the commencement of the Club's playing season (or such subsequent date as the Player's services may commence) and end with the termination of the Club's scheduled playing season, and shall be payable in semi-monthly installments as above provided.

If the Player is in the service of the Club for part of the playing season only, he shall receive such proportion of the salary above mentioned, as the number of days of his actual employment bears to the number of days in the Club's playing season.

Loyalty   3. (a) The Player will faithfully serve the Club or any other Club to which, in conformity with the agreements above recited, this contract may be assigned, and pledges himself to the American public to conform to high standards of personal conduct, of fair play and good sportsmanship.

(b) The Player represents that he does not, directly or indirectly, own stock or have any financial interest in the ownership or earnings of any Major League club, except as hereinafter expressly set forth, and covenants that he will not hereafter, while connected with any Major League club, acquire or hold any such stock or interest except in accordance with Section 23 (e), Article II, Major League Rules.

Service   4. (a) The Player agrees that, while under contract or reservation, he will not play baseball (except post-season games as hereinafter stated) otherwise than for the Club or a Club assignee hereof; that he will not engage in professional boxing or wrestling; and that, except with the written consent of the Club or its assignee, he will not engage in any game or exhibition of football, basketball, hockey, or other athletic sport.

Post-season Games   (b) The Player agrees that, while under contract or reservation, he will not play in any post-season baseball games except in conformity with the Major League Rules; and that he will not play in any such baseball game after October 31st any year until the following training season, or in which more than two other players of the Club participate, or with or against any ineligible player or team.

Assignment   5. (a) In case of assignment of this contract to another Club, the Player shall promptly report to the assignee club within 72 hours from the date he receives written notice from the Club of such assignment, if not more than 1600 miles by most-direct available railroad route, plus an additional 24 hours for each additional 800 miles; accrued salary shall be payable when he so reports; and each successive assignee shall become liable to the Player for his salary during his term of service with such assignee, and the Club shall not be liable therefor. If the Player fails to report as above specified, he shall not be entitled to salary after the date he receives written notice of assignment. If the assignee is a member either of the National or American League, the salary shall be as above (paragraph 2) specified. If the assignee is any other Club the Player's salary shall be the same as that usually paid by said Club to other players of like ability.

Termination (b) This contract may be terminated at any time by the Club or by any assignee upon ten days' written notice to the Player.

Regulations 6. The Player accepts as part of this contract the Regulations printed on the third page hereof, and also such reasonable modifications of them and such other reasonable regulations as the Club may announce from time to time.

Agreements and Rules 7. (a) The Major and Major-Minor League Agreements and Rules, and all amendments thereto hereafter adopted, are hereby made a part of this contract, and the Club and Player agree to accept, abide by and comply with the same and all decisions of the Commissioner pursuant thereto.

Publication (b) It is further expressly agreed that, in consideration of the rights and interest of the public, the Club, the League President, and/or the Commissioner may make public the record of any inquiry, investigation or hearing held or conducted, including in such record all evidence or information given, received or obtained in connection therewith, and including further the findings and decisions therein and the reasons therefor.

Renewal 8. (a) On or before February 15th (or if Sunday, then the succeeding business day) of the year next following the last playing season covered by this contract, by written notice to the Player at his address following his signature hereto (or if none be given, then at his last address of record with the Club), the Club or any assignee hereof may renew this contract for the term of that year except that the salary shall be such as the parties may then agree upon, or in default of agreement the Player will accept such salary rate as the Club may fix, or else will not play baseball otherwise than for the Club or for an assignee hereof.

(b) The Club's right of reservation of the Player, and of renewal of this contract as aforesaid, and the promise of the Player not to play otherwise than with the Club or an assignee hereof, have been taken into consideration in determining the salary specified herein and the undertaking by the Club to pay said salary is the consideration for both said reservation, renewal option and promise, and the Player's service.

Disputes 9. In case of dispute between the Player and the Club or any Major League Club assignee hereof, the same shall be referred to the Commissioner as an umpire, and his decision shall be accepted by all parties as final; and the Club and the Player agree that any such dispute, or any claim or complaint by either party against the other, shall be presented to the Commissioner within one year from the date it arose.

Supplemental Agreements 10. The Club and Player covenant that this contract fully sets forth all understandings and agreements between them, and agree that no other understandings or agreements, whether heretofore or hereafter made, shall be valid, recognizable, or of any effect whatsoever, unless expressly set forth in a new or supplemental contract executed by the Player and the Club (acting by its president, or such other officer as shall have been thereunto duly authorized by the president or Board of Directors, in writing filed of record with the League President and Commissioner—and that no other Club officer or employe shall have any authority to represent or act for the Club in that respect), and complying with all agreements and rules to which this contract is subject.

Special Covenants
See "Important Notice" above.

This contract shall not be valid or effective unless and until approved by the League President or Advisory Council, as the case may be.

Signed in duplicate this......*15th*...... day of ....*January*........., A. D. 193.*1*.

[SEAL]

AMERICAN BASE BALL CLUB OF PHILADELPHIA
.... (Club)

Witness: By .....*John D. Shibe*......
                                                   (President)
...*Robert Schroeder*...   ...*Robert M. Grove*...
                                                   (Player)

.... (Home address of Player)

REGULATIONS

1. The Club's playing season for each year covered by this contract and all renewals hereof shall be as fixed by the American League of Professional Baseball Clubs, or, if this contract shall be assigned to a Club in another league, then by the league of which such assignee is a member.

2. The Player must keep himself in first-class physical condition and must at all times conform his personal conduct to standards of good citizenship and good sportsmanship.

3. The Player, when requested by the Club, must submit to medical examination at the expense of the Club and, if necessary, to treatment by a regular physician in good standing at the Player's expense. Disability directly resulting from injury sustained in playing baseball for the Club while rendering service under this contract shall not impair the right of the Player to receive his full salary for the season in which the injury was sustained, but only upon the express, prerequisite condition that written notice of such injury, including the time, place, cause and nature of the injury, is served upon and received by the Club within twenty days of the sustaining of said injury. Any other disability may be ground for suspending or terminating this contract at the discretion of the Club.

4. The Club will furnish the Player with two complete uniforms, exclusive of shoes, the Player making a deposit of $30.00 therefor, which deposit will be returned to him at the end of the season or upon the termination of this contract, upon the surrender of the uniforms by him to the Club.

5. The Club will provide and furnish the Player while "abroad," or traveling with the Club in other cities, with proper board, lodging, and pay all proper and necessary traveling expenses, including Pullman accommodations and meals en route.

6. For violation by the Player of any regulation the Club may impose a reasonable fine and deduct the amount thereof from the Player's salary or may suspend the Player without salary for a period not exceeding thirty days, or both, at the discretion of the Club. Written notice of the fine or suspension or both and of the reasons therefor shall in every case be given to the Player.

7. In order to enable the Player to fit himself for his duties under this contract, the Club may require the Player to report for practice at such places as the Club may designate and to participate in such exhibition contests as may be arranged by the Club for a period of ....fifty............... days prior to the playing season without any other compensation than that herein elsewhere provided, the Club, however, to pay the traveling expenses, including Pullman accommodations, and meals en route, of the Player from his home city to the training place of the Club, whether he be ordered to go there direct or by way of the home city of the Club. In the event of the failure of the Player to report for practice or to participate in the exhibition games, as provided for, he shall be required to get in playing condition to the satisfaction of the Club's team manager, and at the Player's own expense, before his salary shall commence.

AMERICAN LEAGUE
PLAYER'S CONTRACT

The_____

AMERICAN BASE BALL CLUB
OF PHILADELPHIA,
21st Street & Lehigh Avenue,
(Club)

Of_____

WITH

Robert M. Grove,
(Player)

Lonaconing, Md.

Of_____

Approved:

E S Barnard

President, American League of Professional Baseball Clubs

FEB - 7 1931

_____, 193___

On the following page is a menu from the train carrying the 1929 Philadelphia Athletics from Chicago to Philadelphia. The powerful A's, led by Lefty Grove, Jimmie Foxx, Al Simmons, and catcher Mickey Cochrane, had just won the first two games of the 1929 World Series against the Cubs. These were the days of long train rides through open fields, with card games and baseball banter. The menu was signed by all the A's players, team executives, coaches, and their wives—sixty-six people associated with the team.

MENU

Philadelphia Athletics

American League Champions

Special Train

Enroute Chicago to Philadelphia

October, 1929

PENNSYLVANIA RAILROAD

SPECIAL DINNER $1.25

Please Write on Meal Check "Special Dinner" and Each Item Desired

Cream of Cauliflower

Broiled Whitefish, Maitre d'Hotel
Saute Potatoes   Tomato, Mayonnaise

or

Omelet with Creamed Chicken and Mushrooms
Julienne Potatoes   Green Peas

or

Breaded Rack Lamb Chops, Tomato Sauce
Hashed in Cream Potatoes   New Lima Beans

or

Roast Loin of Pork with Dressing, Green Apple Sauce
Mashed Potatoes   Baked Hubbard Squash

or

Vegetarian Dinner with Poached Egg;

Includes Assorted Bread; Pot of Coffee or Tea, or
Bottle of Sweet Milk or Buttermilk

SPECIALTIES

Cream of Cauliflower—Cup 30, Tureen 45
Celery 35   Young Onions 25   Radishes 25
Broiled Whitefish, Maitre d'Hotel 80
Fried Lake Trout, Tartar Sauce 80
Creamed Chicken a la King with New Peas 1.10
Sirloin Steak, Minute, au Gratin Potatoes,
Lettuce and Tomato Salad 1.50
Mixed Grill (Rack Lamb Chop, Bacon, Fresh Mushrooms)
with Long Branch Potatoes 1.25
Fresh Lima Beans 40   Baked Hubbard Squash 30   New Peas 40
Potatoes—Mashed 30   Long Branch 35   Hashed in Cream 35
Saute 35
Whole Tomato, Mayonnaise 45
Green Apple Pie 25; with Cheese 35
French Vanilla Ice Cream with Sliced Peaches 45
Cream Cheese with Bar-le-duc Jelly, Toasted Rye Bread 60
Honeydew Melon 40
Sliced Peaches with Cream 45   Grapefruit, Half 35
Baked Apple with Cream 35

DINNER A LA CARTE

Soups
Cup 30; Tureen 45
Clam Chowder; Consomme

Relishes
Sweet Pickles 30
Ripe, Green or Stuffed Olives 25 Tomato or Sauerkraut Juice 25

Fish
See Specialties

Grilled
Rack Lamb Chop 65   Sirloin Steak 1.75
Young Chicken (Half) 1.25
Ham or Bacon and Eggs 80
Ham 80; Half Portion 45
Bacon 80; Half Portion 45; Per Slice 15

Eggs and Omelets
Eggs—Boiled, Fried, Shirred or Scrambled (1) 30; (2) 40
Poached on Toast 50   Omelet, Plain 60

Cold Meats, Etc.
Assorted Cuts 1.25; Ham 85
Sliced Breast of Chicken 1.25
Roast Beef 1.00   Ox Tongue 90
Pickled Pigs' Feet, Cold Slaw 80
(Potato Salad Served With Cold Meats)
French Sardines 65   Baked Beans (Hot or Cold) 45

Sandwiches
Cold Roast Beef 50   Ham 30   Ox Tongue 30
American Cheese 30   Chicken Mayonnaise 50
Chicken Salad 50; on Toast with Sliced Tomato 75
Fried Egg 35   Fried Ham 45   Fried Ham and Egg 55

Vegetables
Potatoes: French Fried 35; Hashed Browned 35
Stewed Tomatoes 30   String Beans 30

Salads
With Saltine Wafers and French, Mayonnaise or Thousand Island
Dressing; Head Lettuce 40; with Tomato 50; Combination 60;
with Roquefort or Pennsylvania Dressing 25 cents extra
Chicken 1.00   Potato 40
Asparagus Chiffonade 50

Bread, Etc.
Vienna, Raisin, Graham, Brown or Rye 15
Toast, Dry or Buttered 20; Milk 35; Cream 50
Bran Cookies 15   Whole Wheat Wafers 15   Crackers 10

Desserts and Fruit
Steamed Fig Pudding, Hard and Fruit Sauce 35
Ice Cream 35   Wafers 15
Bar le duc 35   Hawaiian Pineapple 35
Preserved Figs in Syrup 50   Raw Apple 15   Orange 20; Sliced 30
Orange Marmalade or Strawberry Preserves (Individual) 35

Cheese with Crackers
Imperial 30   Swiss Gruyere 35
Roquefort 40   Camembert 35
Yeast Cake and Crackers 10

Coffee, Tea, Etc.
Coffee, Pot for One 25; Demi Tasse 15
Tea, Pot for One 25; Cocoa, Pot for One 30
Kaffee Hag (Pot) 35   Instant Postum (Pot) 30
Milk (Individual Bottle) 20   Cream, per Glass 35
Buttermilk (Pint) 20   Malted Milk, Hot or Cold 30

A service charge of 25c will be made for each person served outside of dining car.
Pay only upon presentation of check; see that extensions and total are correct.

Jimmie Foxx   George Earnshaw

Ida V. Shibe   Mrs. J. D. Shibe

Bing Miller

B. McClork   Mrs. R. W. Oberholtzer

Jimmy Dykes   Mr. & Mrs. S. Harding

Bevo LeBourveau   Paul Mcgottlieb

Earle Mack

Jim Cronin   R. J. Ohl

L. J. Jones   Al. Simmons

Cy Perkins

Rachel Perkins   Homer Summa

Joe Boley   Lefty Yerkes

Max. Bishop

Thos. Shibe

Sam Hale   Lois H. Herb

Alma Hale

Tommy Richardson

George Burns   Jake H. Collins

Eloy Mattox   Bennie Head

Arthur Brown

Charles Harding   Emma Rommel

Harry W. Mackey

108

SATCHEL PAIGE

Born 1906, Mobile, Alabama. Died 1982, Kansas City, Missouri. Paige pitched for forty-two years, in over 2,500 games for over 250 teams (many of them one-day employers), earning approximately 2,000 victories with 100 no-hitters. At forty-two, he was the oldest rookie in major league baseball, helping the Cleveland Indians to a last world championship, in 1948, by winning 6 and losing 1, with a 2.48 ERA. Joe DiMaggio, Dizzy Dean, and Charlie Gehringer called Paige the greatest pitcher they had ever seen. He was the first of the Negro league ballplayers to be admitted into the Hall of Fame in 1972.

PAIGE

HE BEGAN WORK CARRYING SUITCASES AT MOBILE UNION STATION AND DE-VISED A SLING HARNESS FOR HUSTLING SEVERAL BAGS AT ONCE. THE OTHER RED CAPS SAID HE LOOKED LIKE A "WALKING SATCHEL TREE" THUS LEROY BECAME SATCHEL. AND SATCHEL BECAME A LEGEND.

HOW TO STAY YOUNG

1 AVOID FRIED MEATS WHICH ANGRY UP THE BLOOD.
2 IF YOUR STOMACH DISPUTES YOU, LIE DOWN AND PACIFY IT WITH COOL THOUGHTS.
3 KEEP THE JUICES FLOWING BY JANGLING AROUND GENTLY AS YOU MOVE.
4 GO VERY LIGHT ON THE VICES, SUCH AS CARRYING ON IN SOCIETY. THE SOCIAL RAMBLE AIN'T RESTFUL.
5 AVOID RUNNING AT ALL TIMES.
6 DON'T LOOK BACK. SOMETHING MIGHT BE GAINING ON YOU.

The headstone on Satchel's grave (inset) gives his prescription for a long life.

C.J. NITKOWSKI

Born 1973, Suffern, New York. C.J. has been an effective left-handed reliever from 1995 to the present with the Reds, Tigers, and Astros. In 1994, while pitching in the minors, he had the rare opportunity to pitch to one of history's greatest athletes, Michael Jordan, who had just quit basketball to try his hand at baseball. **I ASKED C.J. WHAT IT WAS LIKE TO FACE THE LIVING LEGEND THAT IS MICHAEL JORDAN.**

Mighty Michael at the bat, 1994

Seth,

I faced Michael Jordan 5 times in 1994 when he was playing AA baseball for the Birmingham Barons and I was a member of the Chattanooga Lookouts (Cincinnate Reds affiliate). I can honestly say in my entire baseball career, he was the guy who stands out the most. Obviously not for his baseball talent, but more so for the thrill of competing against possibly the greatest athlete that ever lived.

I went into the game thinking 'no big deal', just another guy I have to get out. When I got to the mound and he came up , that feeling quickly changed. It was probably the only time in my career I ever had to step back for a minute and say to myself, "Wow, I cannot believe I am here!"

After two pitches, I needed to gear my attention to the task at hand, getting MJ out! The first two times around I was unsuccessful; I walked him twice. I had three friends drive 17 hours from New York to see me face the great MJ. They had a great time.

All in all Jordan went 0 for 2 against me with 2 strikeouts and 3 walks. He happened to hit one of his three career home runs that first night I faced him, but not, thank God!, off me (I would have never heard the end of that).

I also got an MJ autograph for myself, and I treasure it dearly, because it represents a snapshot in my career. I just hope after I'm long gone, my great grand-kids can appreciate that moment like I did.

C.J. Nitkowski
10-23-97

Bucky chooses Mickey Rivers' bat over his own.

MIKE TORREZ

Born 1946, Topeka, Kansas. Torrez played from 1967 to 1984, winning 185 games. He was a solid right-hander who, during his prime, averaged over 15 wins a year. Pitching for the Red Sox against the Yankees in a one-game play-off to determine the Eastern Division championship on October 2, 1978, he surrendered the crushing (to Red Sox fans) seventh-inning home run to light-hitting shortstop Bucky Dent. The stunning blow recalled Bobby Thomson's "Shot Heard Round the World," the home run that decided the 1951 Giants-Dodgers play-off series. Ironically, the man who gave up Thomson's shot, Ralph Branca, and Torrez both at one time, attended the same church in White Plains, New York, Our Lady of Sorrows.

I ASKED TORREZ IF HE EVER TALKS TO HIS OLD TEAMMATE BUCKY DENT ABOUT THAT HOME RUN.

Torrez throws the pitch that sank Boston hearts.

Dear Seth,

The 1978 Yankees/Red Sox playoff game was truly a memorable moment in baseball, especially for me as the losing pitcher of record.

I really don't think about it unless it is mentioned (which is quite often.)

For me this is positive, as it has kept my name in baseball, via newspapers & T.V. People tend to forget my great "77" playoff and 2 - World Series games wins for the Yanks! When Bucky Dente's new stadium opened in Florida, we re-enacted that all too familiar pitch. It took him 20 swings just to hit it out of the "Little Green Monster" in Florida.

Even today we see each other several times a year.

I kid him alot about using a cork-bat (Mickey Rivers bat). I will tell you this, all those Yankees used to Cork (Ha-Ha).

Take Care
Mike Torrez

JOSE LIMA

Born 1972, Santiago, Dominican Republic. The 1998 baseball season was highlighted by many seemingly unimaginable records being broken, tied, or set: the New York Yankees winning 125 baseball games, Kerry Wood striking out twenty in a game, Cal Ripken Jr. ending his consecutive games-played streak at 2,632.

But the story of the year was the electrifying home-run race between St. Louis Cardinal Mark McGwire and Chicago Cub Sammy Sosa, in pursuit of the single-season home-run record. McGwire took a huge early lead, 24–9, before Sosa went on a home-run-hitting barrage in June (he hit 20 that month, a record for most in a month), propelling him back into the race. By mid-September, they had both broken Maris's record. Sosa then took the lead in the dramatic race (for all of fifty-seven minutes) when he hit his 66th and final home run of the year, on September 25, off Houston Astro pitcher Jose Lima. Lima, a highly regarded salsa singer in the off-season, was also having a terrific year, compiling a 16–8 won-lost record. **I ASKED JOSE WHAT GIVING UP A HISTORIC HOME RUN FEELS LIKE.**

Sammy's 66th

If doesn't FEEL good because ; ALREADY gave up #50
AND 51 BACK IN chicago AND every body said that
i grooved" it To him. I KNOW IN MY HEART. I didn't
AND thats ALL that MATTERS TO ME ..
when SAMMY hit #66, I WAS MAD At MYSELF
because I dont want PEOPLE TO SAY the
SAME thing AGAIN. WHEN I FACED
McGwire I CHALLENGED him. I Pitched
the SAMEWAY I do To everybody. NO ONE
SCARES ME. IVE BEEN pitching like that
ALL MY LIFE.
" NO TWO PEOPLE ARE MORE dESERVING OF
bREAKING the RECORD thAN MARK McGwire
AND SAMMY SOSA .. Att José Lima

HOUSTON ASTROS BASEBALL CLUB
P.O. BOX 288 • HOUSTON, TEXAS 77001-0288 • 713-799-9500
BASEBALL ADMINISTRATION Fax 713-799-9562 • MARKETING Fax 713-799-9794 • TICKET SERVICES Fax 713-799-9812

NATIONAL LEAGUE WEST CHAMPIONS
1980   1986

NATIONAL LEAGUE CENTRAL CHAMPIONS
1997   1998

ROBIN ROBERTS

Born 1926, Springfield, Illinois. A fastballer, he was the winningest pitcher in baseball's golden decade, the 1950s, with 199 wins. He dominated that decade, leading both leagues in all the major pitching categories— wins, strikeouts, complete games, innings pitched—at one time or another. Robin ultimately won 286 games in his nineteen-year career (1948–1966) spent mostly with the Philadelphia Phillies and Baltimore Orioles. A Hall of Famer elected in 1976, he always challenged hitters and thus has the dubious distinction of allowing more home runs in his career than any other pitcher in history, with 505. **NO PITCHER LIKES TO GIVE UP HOME RUNS. I ASKED HIM IF SOME OF THE HOMERS HE GAVE UP WERE MORE PAINFUL THAN OTHERS.**

Seth—

The home runs that decided a game caused much anguish — If the home run didn't alter the score it was Just another run —

I had both kinds — Too many in fact! Sorry you mentioned it.

Sincerely,
Robin Roberts

STU MILLER

Born 1927, Northampton, Massachusetts. Stu was an effective relief pitcher for sixteen years (1952–1968) with five teams. On May 14, 1967, at Yankee Stadium, he gave up Mickey Mantle's 500th career home run. Mickey, at the time, was only the sixth player to reach that plateau. He ended up with 536 career home runs.

I ASKED MILLER IF HE REMEMBERED THE PITCH HE THREW THAT THE MICK MADE HISTORY WITH.

MANTLE HIT A 3 AND 2 PITCH THAT WAS A LITTLE LOW AND A LITTLE OUTSIDE — BALL FOUR — IT WAS MY BEST PITCH A STRAIGHT CHANGE-UP. HE HAD TO BE LOOKING FOR IT. I TIP MY HAT TO HIM — A GREAT HITTER.

IT WAS THE ONLY HOME RUN HE HIT OFF ME IN MY FIVE YEARS WITH THE ORIOLES.

Stu Miller

ART DITMAR

Born 1929, Winthrop, Massachusetts. Art won 72 games for three teams in his eight-year career (1954–1962). In 1960 he was the ace of the pennant-winning New York Yankees. That year's World Series featured Bill Mazeroski's dramatic, bottom-of-the-ninth, Series-winning home run. In 1985, Anheuser-Busch ran a beer commercial on television featuring the original call of Maz's home run by announcer Chuck Thompson, who mistakenly identified Ditmar as the man who surrendered it. Ditmar did not even play in that game and asked Anheuser-Busch to excise his name from the ad. When they refused, he sued them for $3.5 million, claiming his reputation had been damaged. **I ASKED HIM WHAT THE RESULT OF HIS LAWSUIT WITH ANHEUSER-BUSCH WAS.**

Dear Seth,

In regard to the law suit I had with Anheuser-Busch beer regarding their bogus commercial back in 1985 was eventually thrown out of Court but did reach the Supreme Court.

The Judge in Cleveland felt that 'throwing a home run ball' was 'not that big a deal' so she threw the case out.

I still feel that no company has a right to misuse your name in a situation they knew was incorrect.

Thank you for your interest,

Art Ditmar

BALOR MOORE

Born 1951, Smithville, Texas. A left-hander, Balor pitched for nine seasons (1970, 1972–1974, 1977–1980), mostly with the Montreal Expos and Toronto Blue Jays. On September 16, 1972, in Philadelphia, he surrendered the first home run hit by a rookie third baseman named Mike Schmidt. Schmidt went on to hit 547 more and is generally acknowledged as the greatest third baseman in the game's history.

I ASKED BALOR TO RECOUNT HIS ENCOUNTER WITH THE GREAT POWER HITTER.

3/30/98

I remember Mike Schmidt's 1st home run very well. The story goes like this:

I was a rookie in '72 and had been pitching very well at the time. My previous 2 starts had been shut outs against the Mets and the Pirates plus a few more innings against the Braves. We were leading the Phillies going into the bottom of the 8th by 1-0. Philly had loaded the bases with no outs. I remember thinking about the situation but pitching as well as I had been at the time I thought I still could escape the inning. The 4th hitter of the inning hit a liner to Foli @ short who dove to his left making the catch and flipping to 2nd for a double play, the runner at 3rd holding. Now we have 1st & 3rd, 2 outs and a pinch hitter is announced. I look at the scoreboard and see it is a guy named Schmidt, just called up from the minors. The catcher, I remember it being Bocabella but Tim McCarver remembers catching that game, comes to the mound and ask what I know about Schmidt? We decide not to get beat on anything but my fastball. After 2 pitches we have the count in our favor 0-2 and call for a fastball low & away. Good call, bad pitch. Normally my fastball away will tail off the plate but in this instance it started low & away and ran back over the heart of the plate.

As I faced Schmidt many more times this was a pitch I found he could hit and hit very far, which he did that Sept. nite at the Vet. On that pitch the Phillies went on to win 3-2, my consecutive scoreless streak ended at 27+ innings and Mike Schmidt hit his 1st big league home run.

Balor Moore

Michael Jack Schmidt

JIM BOUTON

Born 1939, Newark, New Jersey.
Jim won 21 and 18 games respectively, pitching for the 1963 and
1964 New York Yankees. He
also gained notoriety in 1970 as
the author of *Ball Four*, which
honestly chronicled the life
of a major league base-
ball player. Eight years
after his retirement in
1970, Jim learned to
throw the knuckleball
and in 1978, made a
comeback with the
Atlanta Braves. In 29
games in relief, he won
a game and struck out
10 hitters.

**I WONDERED WHAT
IT WAS LIKE TRYING A
COMEBACK SO MANY
YEARS AFTER THROWING
HIS LAST PITCH.**

Jim Bouton

October 8, 1998

Dear Seth,

Making a comeback to the big leagues with the Braves in 1978 was a lot harder than making it the first time with the Yankees in 1962 - I was 39, hadn't pitched in the big leagues for 8 years, and my main pitch was a knuckleball. And I was far more nervous with the comeback because some people said it was just a stunt, including some of the players. Which is why beating the Giants 4-1 during their pennant race in '78 was more fun than winning a World Series game.

And can you believe I was Giant's fan when I was a kid? Used to watch them play in the old Polo Grounds. I could imitate every player's batting stance.

Sincerely,

Jim Bouton

DON LIDDLE

Born 1925, Mount Carmel, Illinois.
Don pitched from 1953 to 1956 with
the New York Giants and two other
teams, finishing his career with a
28–18 won-lost record. The powerful
Cleveland Indians of 1954, with their
111 regular-season victories, were a
lock to win that year's World Series
against the New York Giants. In the
bottom of the eighth, in Game One,
with the score tied at two and two men
on, Liddle came in to face Cleveland's
slugging first baseman Vic Wertz.
Wertz blasted a 440-foot shot to center field, where Willie Mays made a
spectacular over-the-shoulder catch—
known now simply as "The Catch"—to
preserve the tie. The Giants ended up
winning the contest on Dusty Rhodes's
home run in the tenth and went on to
sweep the Tribe, stunning the baseball
world. Don also was the starting and
winning pitcher in the final game of
that Series. **I WONDERED IF HE
REMEMBERED THE DETAILS THAT LED
TO "THE CATCH."**

Seth,

The situation in the First game of the World Series, was a relief Pitcher's nightmare. Men on First & second and nobody out. Freddie Fitzsimons was the one who was on the Mound waving me into the ball game. When I arrived at the Mound he asked me if I remember how they wanted Wertz Pitched, I answered yes, he's a good bow' ball hitter. With nobody out West Westrum our Catcher told me, he may bunt, as there was nobody out.

The First pitch was a high inside fast ball, he, looked at it High, for a ball. now we threw him another fast ball up, but we wanted it away, we caught the outside corner for a strike, now Wes said he'll bunt now. We came back high & tight, he bunted the ball toward the Cleveland dogout. Too good of a hitter to bunt with two strikes so we showed him a curve outside for a ball, came back with a fast ball away and up. he hit it deep to center Field.

After the game in the Club House, I lockered next to Willie, and when Leo Durocher came over the Congratulate Willie on "the Catch," I told Leo well," I got my man," just to belittle the great Catch Willie Made.

Don Liddle

ROLANDO ARROJO

Born 1968, Havana, Cuba. The ace of the expansion Tampa Bay Devil Rays, Rolando won 14 games and came in second in the 1998 balloting for American League Rookie of the Year. A great pitcher for the Cuba National Team (160–80 won-lost record), he defected to the United States in July of 1996. Although he officially does not speak English, Rolando has been seen reading the sports pages of English-speaking newspapers after games he's pitched. **I ASKED HIM TWO UNRELATED QUESTIONS:**

WHETHER IT WAS CONVENIENT NOT TO SPEAK ENGLISH SOMETIMES,

AND WHETHER HIS MOTHER

WAS INVOLVED

IN HIS BASEBALL

CAREER.

December 3, 1998

Not knowing English is difficult and it is not convenient. You never know how you are being judged, good or bad, and you're always "up in the air" as to what is happening in your surroundings. I've been told, however, that sometimes, it is convenient not to know English.

My mother never played baseball with me, but I do believe that she played a very important part in my career with the guidance I received from her as a child. She always pushed me to do my best at the game. She felt my pain with any loss or defeat, even though she never showed it, but I knew. She always said to me: "Everything happens for a reason."

Es dificil no saber Ingles y no es conveniente pues nunca sabes como te juzgan, si bieno mal y siempre te quedas en el aire sin saber nada de lo que está pasando a tu alrededor. Y también me han contado que en muy pocas ocaciones, si es conveniente no saber Ingles.

Mi madre nunca jugó conmigo al beisbol, pero si creo que fué muy importante en mi carrera, por la educación que me dio siendo joven, y siempre te ponia el maximo esfuerzo al juego, pues ella sufria mis DERROTAS, aunque nunca me lo demostro, siempre me decia y aun me dice "To lo que sucede conviene."

MAX LANIER

Born 1915, Denton, North Carolina. Max was the St. Louis Cardinal's key left-hander in the 1940s, helping pitch them to two world championships in three years (1942 and 1944). In 1946, when Mexican entrepreneur Jorge Pasquel started raiding the major leagues for talent for his Mexican League, his biggest catch was Max, who had won 45 games over the previous three years. With the Cardinals, Max was making $10,000 a year, but Pasquel's offer of $135,000 over five years was too good to pass up. Pasquel's brother-in-law, Miguel Alemán, was a candidate for the presidency of Mexico in 1946, and Pasquel's recruitment of major-league players to play in Mexico that season helped to elect him easily. Most every major leaguer returned quickly to the majors because of the poor conditions in Mexico. **I ASKED MAX WHAT IT WAS LIKE PLAYING BASEBALL IN MEXICO IN THE 1940s.**

Dec, 30, 1996

Dear, Mr. Swirsky,

I couldn't believe Baseball conditions could be so different until I got to Mexico. They had wonderful fans but terrible fields. We had a railroad track in between the out field & infield & when the train went through they had to open the gates for it to go through.

It was really hard to throw a curve ball in Mexico City & Puebla because of the high altitude.

In 1946 it was election time in Mexico & "Aliman" was running for president & he was the owner- "George Pasquel's" bro. law. That is the reason Pasquel got us the fans love baseball & they voted for "Aliman". Even our clubhouse man said he voted seven times.

Sincerely,
Max Lanier

125

AL PRATT

Born 1848, Allegheny, Pennsylvania. Died 1937, Pittsburgh, Pennsylvania. Al was the starting and losing pitcher in baseball's first official major-league game, played May 4, 1871. The game between Al's Cleveland Forest Grays and the Fort Wayne Kekiongas also resulted in baseball's first shutout. In 1918, Al wrote down many of his experiences in a fascinating diary that offers a unique insight into life and baseball in the 1860s and 1870s.

The Cleveland Forest Grays, 1871. Al is holding the ball.

On the following pages are a few passages from Al's diary, including his account of how he and his catcher Jim "Deacon" White invented the catcher's mitt.

From my earliest recollection I had a ball. In 1858. I played my first base-ball, and cricket. with the boys on the Commons of Allegheny and played until July 14. 1864 my base-ball career being cut short by enlisting in the Civil War in the one hundred day service with Captain James Crow- Company G. - 193rd. Pennsylvania Volunteers. I returned home, in the late part of November, and in the last call of President Lincoln, in February for volunteers to serve one year — during the war, I reenlisted. In 1867

I went all through that Campaign to the surrender of Lee at Appomattox. From Appomattax we marched to intercept Gen. Johnston in N.C. and here I know to play a little more base - ball —

This small "lemon peel" ball is the kind they played with in the 1800s.

I started in as pitcher of the Enterprise — then the leading club of Western Pennsylvania, and in that year our regular team never lost but one game. In this same year I received my first salary as a base ball player. My salary amounting to the enormous sum of ten dollars a week.

Old 'Deacon White' and I made the first glove ever used on the ball field, in 1870. Made from buck-skin driving glove. We were in N-Y at the time. White's hands were so sore he could not catch. We went down Broadway one day to a wholesale house and the only thing we could find suitable was a pair of heavy buck gauntlet gloves. We took these, cut the gauntlets off, cut the fingers out and took them to a tailors to put a little padding in the hand. We were playing the Mutuals of New York, and White came on the grounds with the gloves on. The crowd started to yell "take the gloves off- take the gloves off" and the Mutuals protested to the umpires against White wearing the gloves. — The umpires decided that their was nothing in the rules to prohibit White from wearing the gloves, and Jim caught through the game although it took him some little time to get accustomed so he could hold the ball. It was not a great while until all the catchers were getting protection for their hands.

Baseball's First Shutout Game in Box Score Form

Kekionga.	R.	H.	P.	A.	Forest, Cl	R.	H.	P.	A.
Williams, 3	0	2	2	0	JWhite, c..	0	3	9	0
Mathews, p	0	0	1	0	Kimball, 2..	0	0	4	0
Foran, 1...	0	1	2	0	Pabor, l...	0	0	0	0
G'smith, s.	0	0	3	1	Allison, m.	0	1	2	0
Lennon, c..	1	1	9	1	WWhite, r..	0	0	1	0
Carey, 2..	0	0	4	0	Pratt, p....	0	0	1	0
Mincher, l.	0	0	4	0	Sutton, 3..	0	1	0	1
McD'ott, m	0	1	0	1	Carleton, 1.	0	0	6	0
Kelly, r....	1	1	2	0	Bass, s....	0	0	1	4
Totals...	2	6	27	3	Totals...	0	5	24	5

Kekionga	...0	1	0	0	1	0	0	0	0—2
Forest City	..0	0	0	0	0	0	0	0	0—0

Errors—J. White, Kimball, Allison, Sutton. Double play—Corey (unassisted). Time—2:10. Umpire—J. L. Burke, Cincinnati.

A baseball catcher has a unique view of the game: He's the only player on the field to face the opposite direction of his teammates, his vision is obstructed by the mask he wears, he's the only player not to stand upright, and he must know not only his opponent's tendencies, but his own pitcher's (how fast does he tire, what's his best pitch, etc.). On the following pages are some letters written by or pertaining to catchers.

ED HERRMANN

Born 1946, San Diego, California. A catcher from 1967 to 1978, mostly with the Chicago White Sox, Ed caught one of the best knuckleball pitchers ever, rubber-armed Wilbur Wood. **I ASKED HIM WHAT A TYPICAL CONVERSATION WAS LIKE BETWEEN HIM AND WOOD ON THE MOUND. ED ALSO SHARED A STORY OF HIS INTERESTING RELATIONSHIP WITH THE LATE UMPIRE RON LUCIANO.**

Ed Herrmann

December 10, 1997

Dear Seth,

I had the opportunity to catch a couple of knuckleball pitchers. It was a great time catching Wilbur Wood who had a 24 win 20 loss record in 1973, throwing over 320 innings 4 years in a row! I enjoyed catching him when he pitched BOTH ends of a doubleheader because it required a lot of concentration and stamina.

When I would go out to the mound and talk to Wilbur during the game, we usually talked about fishing. It relaxed him more than anything else. Other pitchers, I might ask them if they saw the beautiful young lady in the 3rd row. I'd talk about anything necessary to loosen them up. Anything to settle a pitcher down was what most converstaions on the mound are geared to.

As an aside, I was the guy that helped umpire Ron Luciano call balls and strikes while I was catching. From an Associated Press article written after they found Luciano dead in his home: "He talked of times he would get catchers to help him call balls and strikes. Ed Herrmann, the former Chicago White Sox catcher, was one of his favorites. "'He was great', Luciano said. 'Most catchers try to steal calls on you, but Ed would be honest with me. If I was under the weather, I'd tell him I needed some help and he'd call them for me. I liked it best when he'd tell me the pitch was out of the strike zone, I'd call it a ball and the pitcher would beef'".

Sincerely,

Ed Herrmann
Scout: Kansas City Royals

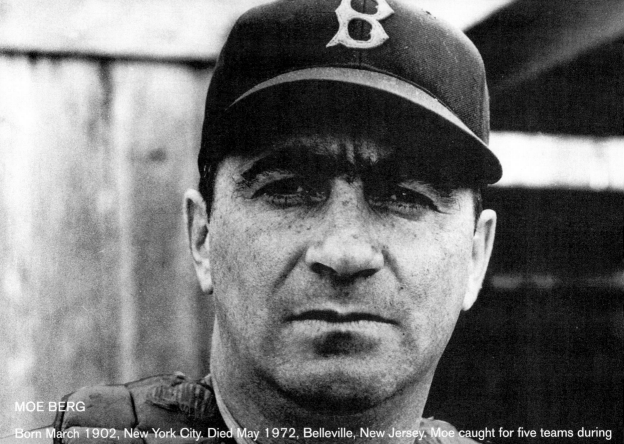

MOE BERG

Born March 1902, New York City. Died May 1972, Belleville, New Jersey. Moe caught for five teams during a fifteen-year career that spanned 1923 through 1939. It was Moe about whom scout Mike Gonzalez coined the phrase "Good field, no hit," when scouting Berg for the Cardinals in the early twenties. Berg only hit .243 in his career but was unlike any ballplayer that ever took the field: He was a master of twelve languages ("he couldn't hit in any one of them," observed teammate Ted Lyons), graduated from Princeton University and Columbia Law School, studied philology at the Sorbonne and was a spy for the United States government before and during World War II.

The document on the following page is orders from the OSS (the precursor to the CIA) to Berg to capture German scientist Werner Heisenberg, head of the Nazi atomic bomb effort. After the war, Berg rarely spoke of his secret activities. But in the late 1960s, out of financial necessity, he agreed to write a book. Berg canceled the project when the young editor assigned to him praised his movies, mistakenly thinking he was about to sign Moe of the Three Stooges.

OFFICE OF STRATEGIC SERVICES
WASHINGTON, D. C.

14 April 1944

MEMORANDUM TO Mr. Morris Berg

SUBJECT: Orders

    You are hereby authorized and directed
to proceed to the destinations indicated in your
invitational Army orders, where you will report
on your arrival to the respective Strategic Services Officers for the purpose of performing the
duties assigned to you by this Agency.

William J. Donovan
Director, OSS

133

"KIng" Carl Hubbell

HARRY DANNING

Born 1911, Los Angeles, California. Harry "The Horse" was the catcher for the powerful New York Giants from 1933 until 1942. A four-time All-Star (1938–1941), he put the target down for the great Hall-of-Fame screwball artist Carl Hubbell. Hubbell was the premier pitcher in the National League in the 1930s, winning 253 games to go with a lifetime 2.98 ERA.

I ASKED HARRY IF HE HAD A STORY THAT DEPICTED CARL HUBBELL'S GREAT CONTROL.

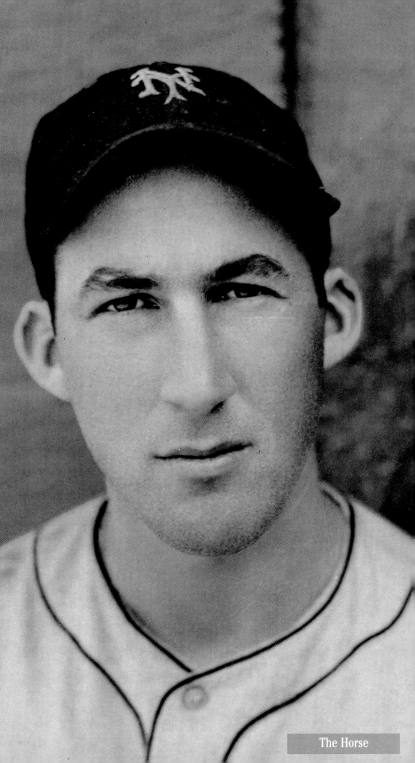

The Horse

Dear Seth:

The Giants were playing in
Boston, a day game, and after,
Carl Hubbell, Mel Ott, Mark Koening
and myself decided to go to the
Dog Track at Revere Beach — we
took a train and arrived a
little early for the track, so
decided to go to the Boardwalk
at Revere —

While wandering through, we
came upon a game — where a
girl in a bathing suit sat
on a piece of wood over a
large vat of water — the object
being if you hit the 'Bull-
Eye' the board would release
and the girl would fall
into the water —

I took my turn — Mel his,
and Mark his and now it
was Carl's turn — He hit
the 'Bulls-eye' so many times
in a row, that the poor
girl quit and wouldn't sit
on the board anymore — I think
this story tells you more about
the Control that Carl had in
his days in the majors —

Sincerely,
Jerry

MILT MAY

Born 1950, Gary, Indiana. Milt caught in 1,034 games over a fifteen-year career spent with five teams. At 12:32 P.M. on May 4, 1975, he drove in major-league baseball's one millionth run.

I ASKED HIM WHO SURRENDERED THAT HISTORIC RUN BATTED IN.

Seth,

The pitcher was John "the count" Montefusco

They were counting down on the scoreboard at Candlestick the number of runs needed to be the millionth. I understand they were doing that in all the ballparks. I, casually watched as the game went on and the number changed quickly 23... 17... 15... etc.

I was in the on deck circle and it was 7, 5 or something and Bob Watson hit a double. As I stepped into the batters box it clicked to one. The first pitch from John Montefusco was a low fastball and it went out.

Bob Watson sprinted home accounting for the millionth run.

Evidently, Dave Concepcion hit a home run simultaneously with me and sprinted around the bases, but Bob, being on 2nd already, had the jump and scored seconds before. Milt May

Dear Seth,

I was next to Tom House (relive pitcher) inside the bull pen. Tom caught the ball and we ran to home plate and gave Hank the ball.

Times were very tough. Hank was receiving alot of death threats because he was black.

We always had a security guard with us.

One night in Alabama after an exhibition game against Baltimore the security guards told us we couldn't go outside our room because it wasn't safe. We waited a little while and sneaked out the back door and went to eat soul food. Luckily we ended up ok. and nothing happen!

The next morning we arrived in Cincinatti to open the season with the Reds. I ran into Hank and his wife Billy outside the hotel and he told me "Casi, Tomorrow I'm going to tie the record and the next day I'm going to sit out and wait till we get to Atlanta and break the record in the first game. So I get have peace of mind the rest of the season!" In Cincinatti, I went inside the clubhouse to change my shirt and when I came outside Hank was running the bases. He had tied the record and I missed it!

In Atlanta he broke the record Just like he said. He sat out the next day and the following day against the Dodgers he hit #716. I caught it Maganvox paid the Braves a million dollars for all the balls after #715.

Paul Casanova

PAUL CASANOVA

Born 1941, Colón, Cuba. Paul was a solid defensive catcher with the Washington Senators and Atlanta Braves from 1965 to 1974. He was Hank Aaron's roommate the year Hank became baseball's all-time home-run leader.

I ASKED PAUL HOW HE EXPERIENCED HIS ROOMMATE'S

RECORD-BREAKER.

A ball used in the game in which Aaron broke Ruth's record.

JOHNNY ROSEBORO

Born 1933, Ashland, Ohio. Johnny caught in 1,585 games (plus 21 World Series games) during a fourteen-year career (1957–1970) spent most prominently with the Los Angeles Dodgers. On August 22, 1965, during a typically intense pitching match-up between Sandy Koufax and Juan Marichal, the ugliest brawl in baseball history broke out when the usually mellow Marichal hit Roseboro over the head with his bat. Marichal felt that Roseboro was returning the ball to Koufax by way of Marichal's ear in retaliation for some alleged knockdown pitches.

I ASKED ROSEBORO IF HE AND MARICHAL EVER RAN INTO EACH OTHER AFTER THE INCIDENT.

The Brawl

11/12/98

WE MET ABOUT 10 YEARS AFTER THE
FIGHT AT DODGER STADIUM, AN OLD
TIMERS GAME.
HE HAS BECOME A _VERY_ GOOD FRIEND.

John Roseboro

JUAN MARICHAL

Born 1937, Laguna Verde, Dominican Republic. Along with Sandy Koufax and Bob Gibson, the "Dominican Dandy" was one of the great pitchers of his generation, pitching almost exclusively for the San Francisco Giants during his sixteen-year career in the majors (1960–1975). Juan won 20 or more games six times, had a lifetime 243–142 won-lost record, a 2.89 earned run average, and won more games than anyone in the decade of the 1960s (191 wins). He was elected to the Hall of Fame in 1983. The pitching duels between Marichal and Dodger ace Sandy Koufax were legendary, resulting in many 1–0 and 2–1 games.

I ASKED JUAN IF KOUFAX EVER TAUGHT HIM ANYTHING ABOUT HIS CRAFT AMID THE INTENSE GIANTS-DODGERS RIVALRY, AND WHY HE PITCHED SO WELL AGAINST THE DODGERS.

The great Juan Marichal

We talked a few times and he would tell me how to hold the ball to throw his curves. We shared pitching tips everytime we would meet or just talk baseball. We have kept in touch through the years, bumping in to eachother at the Legends of Baseball Circuit as well as at the Hall of Fame induction ceremonies in Cooperstown, New York.

Because I knew I was pitching against the best, and against the Dodgers, that was a team I loved pitching against — because there was always a big crowd and a lot of rivalry between the Giants and the Dodgers

Juan Marichel

MAURY WILLS

Born 1932, Washington, D.C. Maurice Morning Wills was a shortstop, mostly for the Los Angeles Dodgers, from 1959 to 1972. A solid hitter (.281 career batting average and 2,134 hits), he was the premier base stealer in baseball from 1960 to 1965, when he led the league every year in steals. In 1962, he won National League MVP honors for being the first modern-day player to steal over 100 bases (he stole 104). It was Maury's revival of the stolen base as an offensive weapon that paved the way for the eventual all-time stolen-base kings, Lou Brock and Rickey Henderson. I

ASKED HIM WHO WAS THE TOUGHEST PITCHER FOR HIM TO STEAL ON.

Juan Marichal was truly tough for me to steal off. The reason was because he changed his rhythm with consistency. He became tough to "time," and thereby keeping me from getting the jump I wanted. However, I got him anyhow! Larry Jackson was even tougher, yet I tied and broke Ty Cobb's single season record against him, numbers 96 and 97. The key for me was that I stole off the Giants' and Cardinal's catcher and middle infielders (delay steal to break Cobb's record). Pitchers threw at my legs all the time. If they were going to put me on, they wanted me hurting. When not hurting, I immediately stole second and third (on the first two pitches) no matter what the score! Or thrown out trying! I felt defiant!

Maury Wills

Maury Wills

BROOKLYN NATIONAL LEAGUE BASEBALL CLUB

215 MONTAGUE STREET, BROOKLYN 1, NEW YORK

GAMES AT
EBBETS FIELD

March 19, 1957.

Mr. Albert Hirsch,
669 Stone Avenue,
Brooklyn 12, N. Y.

Dear Albert:

I have your letter but I wonder how carefully you read
the newspapers. They very clearly stated that we want to keep
the Dodgers in Brooklyn and were willing to spend $5,000,000 to
do so. Progress, however, has been very slow and we will have
to leave Brooklyn if there is not to be a new stadium when our
present lease runs out.

Thank you for writing.

Yours truly,

Walter F. O'Malley,
President.

WFO'M:EM

WALTER O'MALLEY

This letter, written by Dodger owner Walter O'Malley to a fan in early 1957, spelled out the conflict that

eventually led to the Dodgers' move out of Brooklyn. On October 8, 1957, O'Malley followed through on

his threat and formally announced that the Dodgers had played their final game at Ebbets Field and would

relocate to Los Angeles for the 1958 season. The last game at legendary Ebbets Field was played on

September 24, 1957. The starter for Brooklyn that night, Danny McDevitt, describes that game on the

following page.

DANNY MCDEVITT

Born 1932, New York City. Danny pitched from 1957 to 1962 with four teams, earning a 21–27 record. He made history when he shut out the Pirates 2–0 in the final game at Brooklyn's beloved home park.

I ASKED DANNY WHAT HIS THOUGHTS WERE THEN AND NOW REGARDING THE LAST BASEBALL GAME EVER PLAYED AT EBBETS FIELD.

June 14, 1998

Dear Seth,

At the time, the last game at Ebbets Field on September 24, 1957, where
I was the starting pitcher, was almost an insignificant game. However,
I think over the years, the mystique of the Brooklyn Dodgers has grown.

I think a few players who were part of the 'inner circle', the veterans-
- Erskine, Pee Wee, Duke Snider -- <u>knew</u> it was their last game in
Brooklyn, their last game at 'ol Ebbets Field. Think about it, Hodges
started at third that night. Then after he drove in the second run, Pee
Wee, who was very near the end of his career, which he'd played all for
Brooklyn at Ebbets Field, came in at third to finish the game. Hodges
finished the game at first base. Pee Wee played one more year, 1958 out
in LA and then retired. I think they knew for certain it was "goodbye"
to Brooklyn.

Just a little under 7,000 people came out to the game on account of the
cold, damp weather-- not the kind of weather a pitcher likes. We weren't
in a pennant race, so there was no 'build-up' to the game. The game
meant nothing in the little picture, but in the big picture, it was the
end of something great.

When we got the last out in the top of the ninth I was pretty happy. I
couldn't wait to get in the clubhouse and get my hands on a cold
Schaefer Beer. I had pitched about as well, giving up just five hits,   *as I ever*
all groundball singles, and striking out nine . The game, which began at
8 p.m., was over at 10:03 p.m. Back then the games moved right along,
not like the drawn-out affairs of today.

Looking back, pitching that last game at Ebbets was a good, lucky thing
for a guy who ended up 21-27 lifetime with a 4.40 era. I kept the game
ball that night, I guess I did have <u>some</u> sense of the history of that
final game at the much beloved ballpark.

a brief "update,
I've lived in the same house here in Conyers since 1972. And I still
like my scotch and water from time to time.

Thanks again for your interest in the game we played so long ago.

Sincerely,

Danny McDevitt

145

JOHNNY VANDER MEER

Born 1914, Prospect Park, New Jersey. Died 1997, Tampa, Florida. Ebbets Field was the site of many historic games. On June 15, 1938, Brooklyn fans got a double dose of baseball history; not only was it the first night game played at Ebbets Field, but it was also the occasion of Johnny Vander Meer's second consecutive no-hitter, a feat unlikely ever to be matched. Known as the "Dutch Master," Johnny pitched for thirteen seasons (1937–1943, 1946–1951), mostly for the Cincinnati Reds, compiling a 119–121 won-lost record with a 3.44 ERA. The Brooklyn fans cheered him on all the way that night. In the ninth, he walked the bases loaded, but got Ernie Koy to tap into a force-out at home and Leo Durocher to hit a soft outfield fly to end the contest. In Johnny's next game, he had a no-hitter going into the fourth inning—nearly 22 innings of no-hit ball—before Boston Braves outfielder Debs Garms got a base hit.

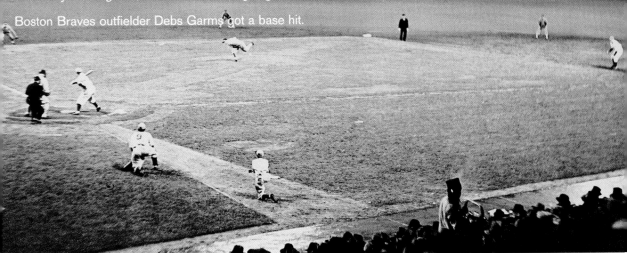

Vander Meer polishes his second gem.

I ASKED JOHNNY WHEN HE KNEW HE HAD THE STUFF TO PITCH THAT SECOND NO-HITTER.

seth –

when warming up to start the game in Brooklyn. I played well when I heard the great Brooklyn fans

Johny Vander Meer

RICHARD W. HALL

I was experimenting with a knuckle ball and it got away

*one wild pitch—
that knuckle ball*

Dick Hall

DICK HALL

Born 1930, St. Louis, Missouri. Hall was an outstanding relief specialist during his career (1955–1971), played mostly with the Pittsburgh Pirates and Baltimore Orioles. His career record was 93–75, with a 3.32 ERA, but his greatest pitching achievement attests to his great control: In the 1,259 innings he pitched over his sixteen-year career, he threw only one wild pitch.

I WONDERED WHAT HAPPENED ON THAT PITCH THAT PREVENTED HIM FROM RECORDING A SPOTLESS CAREER.

147

MARCIA HADDIX

Marcia's husband was Harvey Haddix, a five-foot-nine-and-a-half-inch left-hander who pitched from 1952 to 1965, most notably with the St. Louis Cardinals and Pittsburgh Pirates. Harvey was born in 1925 in Medway, Ohio, and died in 1994 in Springfield, Ohio. On May 26, 1959, "The Kitten," as he was known, pitched what many consider to be the greatest single game in baseball history. He retired thirty-six consecutive Milwaukee Brave batters in a row (a lineup that featured heavy hitters Hank Aaron, Joe Adcock, and Eddie Mathews) through twelve innings, only to lose the game in the thirteenth, 1–0.

I ASKED HARVEY'S WIFE IF HIS REMARKABLE PITCHING PERFOR- MANCE THAT NIGHT WAS THE HIGHLIGHT OF HIS CAREER.

Jan. 14, 1998

Dear Seth,

Most people assume the high-light of Harv's career was the twelve perfect inning game of May 26, 1959, but he wouldn't agree. He felt that game was a loss for his team and he didn't play to lose. Harv, being a team player, maintained the high-light of his career, without question, were the two games he won in the 1960 World Series.

There is no denying the twelve perfect inning game brought Harv lasting notoriety. He always wondered if it would have been as memorable to the public had he won the game!

When Harv was quite ill in Sept. 1991, we read in the newspapers that his Perfect Game was, after 32 years, suddenly declared not a Perfect Game. His friends, his fans, and former colleagues called and wrote to express their indignation. While Harv was comforted by the support he received, the satisfaction in his finest effort was never the same for him.

In his successes and in his failures, Harv was always a winner.

                    Sincerely,
                    Marcia Haddix

MIKE SCOTT

Born 1955, Santa Monica, California. Mike pitched for thirteen years (1979–1991), mostly with the Houston Astros. He was a force on the mound in 1986, winning the Cy Young Award and becoming the only pitcher to clinch a division title with a no-hitter. He then masterfully handcuffed the New York Mets in Games One and Four of the National League Championship Series. Knowing they would have to face the invincible Scott if they lost Game Six, the Mets rallied for three runs in the ninth to tie the contest and ended up winning the game and the series in the sixteenth inning, one of the greatest games played in the post-1969 play-off format. **I ASKED SCOTT IF HE THOUGHT THE METS WERE AFRAID TO FACE HIM IN A POSSIBLE GAME SEVEN.**

I don't think the Mets wanted to go to a 7th game against the Astros that year anything can happen in a 7th game. The Met players were tough and very talented, but what made them special was their resilieng. They showed that in the series against the Astros and the Red Sox

Mike Scott

A ball used by Scott in his division-clinching no-hitter

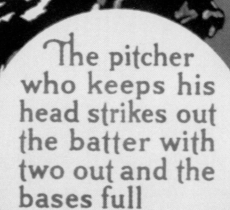

Poster made by Mather & Co., Chicago, 1927

Lazorko "in the nets"

JACK LAZORKO

Born 1956, Hoboken, New Jersey. "Zork" earned a 5–8 record with the California Angels from 1984 to 1988.

I WONDERED IF SKILLS FROM OTHER SPORTS HE PLAYED GROWING UP EVER CAME IN HANDY ON THE MOUND.

There is one game I'll always remember. It was a combination of hockey and pitching. We were playing the Milwaukee Brewers on a hot Sunday afternoon in Anaheim. I came up to the Big Leagues in 1984 with Milwaukee and knew most of the players I was pitching against. They knew fielding was one of my strongest assets. Cecil Cooper hit two shots up the middle. I did the "splits" a hockey term for a goalie, and made a "kick" save early in the game, and a "glove" save late in the game.

I grew up in New Jersey playing hockey every winter between football and baseball season. I enjoyed playing goalie because it would quicken up my glove hand for baseball. I played third base all through high school.

Later in the game, Robin Yount and Paul Molitor hit balls up the middle and I made "glove" saves on both of them. As I turned to get the ball back from Jack Howell I saw all the infielders with their gloves underneath their arms. Dick Schofield yells "Hey Jack, we don't need our gloves anymore, we will just watch you play goalie."

Jack Lazorko

EDDIE O'BRIEN

Born 1930, South Amboy, New Jersey. Eddie has an identical twin brother named Johnnie. Their similarities go beyond their looks: Both were five-foot-nine-inch, 165-pound right-handers, both pitched in a three-year (1956–58) period, both pitched for the Pittsburgh Pirates, and both had one major-league win. Eddie's pitching career consisted of sixteen innings in which he surrendered sixteen hits. Johnnie's numbers were his twin's mirror image as he gave up sixty-one hits in sixty-one innings.

I ASKED EDDIE IF HE AND HIS TWIN EVER PLAYED TRICKS ON OPPOSING TEAMS, AND IF THERE WERE ANY CONSEQUENCES TO THOSE TRICKS.

Seth:

In Spring Training (Ft. Meyers, Fla) we had split squads in the early going. John and I were in different groups. During one exibition game, Ide pinch-hit for Bob Friend in the third inning, changed to my number and pinch hit again in the 7th inning. This was the only time this happened, although we had opponents quite confused when we played basketball.

Sincerely

P.S. Ide struck out for me!

RON REED

Born 1942, LaPorte, Indiana. Ron was a six-foot-six-inch right-hander who pitched from 1966 to 1984 with the Atlanta Braves, Philadelphia Phillies, and two other teams. He won 146 games and was the winning pitcher for the Braves the night his teammate Hank Aaron hit his record-breaking 715th home run. A stand-out basketball player at Notre Dame, he played in the National Basketball Association for Dave DeBusschere's Detroit Pistons from 1965 to 1967, while playing baseball in the summers. He eventually switched solely to baseball in 1968. **I WONDERED WHAT WENT INTO HIS DECISION TO QUIT BASKETBALL FOR BASEBALL.**

Seth;

In basketball you can have longevity if you can do one or two things well. For instance, being a great shooter, or a great rebounder, or a great ball handler. You have to do something well. I felt I didn't have the talent in any one thing to keep my N.B.A. career going very long. Only 11 or 12 players on an N.B.A. team, and every year the first round draft choice makes the team, and a lot of times the second or third round draft choice makes the team; the 'numbers' game can catch up to a 'so-so' player rather quickly. If two new players are coming in the front door, two other players are going out the back door!

Ron Reed

LARRY GOWELL

Born 1948, Lewiston, Maine. Larry pitched in two games for the New York Yankees at the end of the 1972 season, starting and losing one. He also was the last pitcher to get a base hit in the 1972 season. That is significant because the next year in the American League, the designated-hitter rule took effect, eliminating the pitcher's hitting spot. Never adopted by the National League, the DH rule still remains one of the most controversial issues in the game today. **I ASKED LARRY HIS OPINION OF THE DH RULE.**

Thursday, November 27, 1997

Dear Seth:

At the time I felt I was taking something away from the game plus I liked trying to help my own cause at the plate. But looking back over all the years, I think the DH rule has been good for the game because I think people come to ballgames to see runs scored. Very few fans come to the ballpark hoping they will see a 1-0 ballgame with very little hitting. The rule has kept some great hitters in the game much longer, which I think is great.

It certainly takes a lot of pressure off the Manager on whether to leaye the pitcher in the game or pinch hit for him in a tight ballgame -- Managers salaries should have decreased in the American League!

Sincerely Yours,

Larry Gowell

JIM COLBORN

Born 1946, Santa Paula, California. Jim pitched from 1969 to 1978 with the Chicago Cubs, Milwaukee Brewers, and two other teams. His best year was 1973, when he had a 20–12 won-lost record for the Brewers. At the close of the 1976 season, Jim, known as a prankster, disguised himself as the home-plate umpire for that day's game and then proceeded to throw two of his teammates out of the game.

I ASKED HIM TO RECALL THE GREAT PRANK.

Hi Seth –

The Brewers were pretty poor in the early 70's. In the bullpen we would even make up games where our team would be rewarded with a single for any foul ball, a double for a foul ball in the 2nd deck & a triple for a foul ball in the 3rd deck. A H.R. was either a foul ball past the foul pole or a foul over the top of the stadium. In any case we needed goofy stuff like that to stay sane while losing 90 games each year.

I guess that was my idea when I dressed up like the ground crew, visited Bernie Brewer in the beer mug or dressed up like an umpire. Dressing like an umpire was quite effective if I do say so myself. Jim Denkinger, the plate umpire as I recall, allowed me the loan of his outside chest protector and mask. It was the last day of the season and everyone was mostly interested in finishing the game and getting home. I guess we weren't too interested in little details like who was behind the umpire's mask. Alex Grammas, our manager, greeted Ralph Houk with, "You have a nice winter, Ralph." Ralph said, "You too, Alex." I chimed in, "You too, Alex". He half glanced at me, did a double take and bent over laughing. Our bench was loudly, verbally abusing the plate umpire, me, in hopes of getting tossed so they could head home early. I accomodated Ray Sadecki and Gorman Thomas but couldn't really figure out how to throw myself out as I wasn't on the bench.

Sincerely,
Jim Colborn

JON LIEBER

Born 1970, Council Bluffs, Iowa. Jon was a starter on the young and rebuilding Pittsburgh Pirates from 1994 through 1998 until he was traded in the off-season to the Chicago Cubs. Picked to come in last by all the baseball experts in 1997, because of their $9 million payroll (Cecil Fielder of the Yankees made more than the entire Pirates team that year), they gallantly challenged for the top spot in the National League's Central division all year, losing out to the star-laden Houston Astros down the stretch.

I ASKED JON IF PITCHERS STUDY NOT ONLY THE HITTERS ON THE OPPOSING TEAMS, BUT ALSO THE TENDENCIES OF THE HOME-PLATE UMPIRES WHO WILL CALL THEIR GAMES. ALSO, I WONDERED IF HIS TEAMMATES, DESPITE EVERYONE PICKING THEM LAST, WERE CONFIDENT GOING INTO THE '97 SEASON.

PITTSBURGH PIRATES

WORLD CHAMPIONS
1909 ⋄ 1925 ⋄ 1960 ⋄ 1971 ⋄ 1979 ™

PITTSBURGH BASEBALL CLUB
600 Stadium Circle
Pittsburgh, PA 15212
(412) 323-5000
www.pirateball.com

Dear Seth,

As far as studying each homeplate umpires strike zone? Me personally, I think it is a good idea. Just for the fact you can get a feel for where he is going to be the most consistent in the strike zone.

We knew going into the season that we were going to be a team to compete with, no matter what anybody said. We felt like we've got nothing to lose. Everybody deep down inside was very proud, not just of ourselfs, but as a team.

All my best Seth,

#47

Pittsburgh Pirates

159

CLASS OF SERVICE

This is a full-rate Telegram or Cablegram unless its character is indicated by a symbol in the check or in the address.

WESTERN UNION

NEWCOMB CARLTON, PRESIDENT   J. C. WILLEVER, FIRST VICE-PRESIDENT

SYMBOLS

BLUE	Day Letter
NITE	Night Message
NL	Night Letter
LCO	Deferred
CLT	Cable Letter
WLT	Week End Letter

The filing time as shown in the date line on full-rate telegrams and day letters, and the time of receipt at destination as shown on all messages, is STANDARD TIME.

Received at 427 So. LaSalle St., Chicago. Ill.   Telephone—Wabash 4321   1927 JUN 9 AM 4 19

PB70 60 NL.PHILADELPHIA PENN 8

B B JOHNSON,PRES AMERICAN BASEBALL LEAGUE.

    FISHER BLDG CHICAGO ILL.

A FAN SITTING IN FRONT BOX WAS INSULTING GASTON DURING GAM

WHEN TAKEN OUT GASTON PASSING BY ASKED FAN IF HE WAS

TALKING TO HIM HE THEN BECAME MORE ABUSIVE IN HIS LANGUAG

AND GASTON WENT AFTER HIM PLAYERS STOPPED THEM BEFORE ANY

DAMAGE DONE GASTON GOOD LIVING BOY NEED HIM BADLY AS JONE

AND BALLOU OUT FOR SOME TIME.

    DAN P HOWLEY..

MILT GASTON

Born 1896, Ridgefield Park, New Jersey. Died 1996, Hyannis, Massachusetts. A forkball specialist, Milt plied his trade from 1924 through 1934 with five American League teams, compiling a 97—164 won-lost record. He lost 67 more games than he won, a record for pitchers in the twentieth century with over 100 decisions. On June 7, 1927, a fan named Leon Mendel claimed in a letter to American League president Ban Johnson that Gaston, pitching for the St. Louis Browns, went into the stands and roughed him up during a game two days earlier. Browns manager Dan Howley sent Johnson a telegram (above) asking for leniency for his player, but to no avail: Johnson fined Gaston $100 and suspended him for five games.

PHILADELPHIA HAT MANUFACTURING CO.

L. MENDEL & COMPANY

MANUFACTURERS OF

TAILORED AND TRIMMED HATS

704-6-8-10 MARKET STREET

PHILADELPHIA   June 9th 1927.

BELL PHONE, LOMBARD 6820
KEYSTONE PHONE, RACE 1184

Mr. Ban Johnson,
President of the American Baseball League,
Chicago, Ill.,

Dear Sir:-

     I am taking this measure in addressing you as I am the party assaulted by player Gaston, as I do not want the notriety that this player's action has thrust upon me.

     I am not a player baiter and have been a fan all my life and this is the first accasion that I have ever had words or altercation with a player.

     My sole remark to this player,and I can furnish you with any number of witnesses names to vouch for same, was in the third inning while Walberg was being pounded out of the box. Gaston was waiting his turn to bat and laughing good naturedly. I was seated in Box #19 and said to Gaston "Dont laugh you will get yours next innings" and he replied "Yes is that so" After the Athletics went to bat and my prophesy came true, everyone was waving their hands. As Gaston was knocked out of the box he came up to my box and said "What was it you said" and I replied "I said you would get yours and you did" He immediately hit me with his glove and followed this by jumping into my box where he hit me on the arm after trying to take a punch at my face as I supposed he noticed I had a sore eye.

     You evidently noticed that I did not give my name nor have I started any civil or criminal proceedings.

     I am leaving the matter entirely in your hands and hope that Gaston will be treated as severely as a rough-neck player like he deserves.

     Trusting you will keep my name confidential and if you desire I will be only too glad to furnish you with the names of witnesses to substantiate the truth of this episode as I am giving it to you.

     I am,

     Yours respectfully,

Leon Mendel

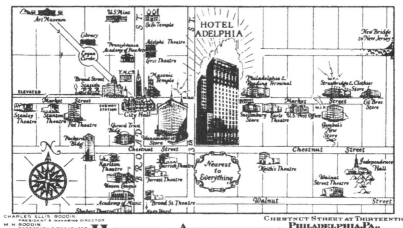

CHARLES ELLIS GOODIN
PRESIDENT & MANAGING DIRECTOR
M. H. GOODIN
SECRETARY & TREASURER

HOTEL ADELPHIA

CHESTNUT STREET AT THIRTEENTH
PHILADELPHIA, PA.,

June 9, 1926

Mr. B. B. Johnson
Chicago, Ill.
Sir:-

Regarding the game of June 7th
in this city during which I was
alleged to have struck a spectator
and for which I received a
suspension I wish to state my
case as follows:- This fan had
been riding me during the entire

game, and after I was knocked from the box in the third inning he used abusive language and became personal. Because the way the game had gone I was hot-tempered enough to go into the stand, but only after he had dared me to do so. I could not say truthfully whether I hit said fan or not I struck at him but it was mostly a battle of words. I realized my mistake a moment after I had entered the stands and left same when ordered to do so by the umpire, Mr. Rowland.

Respectfully yours
Milton Gaston

BILL VEECK

Born 1914, Chicago, Illinois. Died 1986, Chicago, Illinois. Although he'll be remembered as the guy who sent midget Eddie Gaedel to the plate in a 1951 stunt, Veeck was among the most influential and innovative team owners ever. His true love of the game manifested itself in the countless number of fun promotions he sponsored. As the owner of the Cleveland Indians (1946–1949), St. Louis Browns (1951–1953), and Chicago White Sox (1959–1961, 1975–1981) over the course of his nearly sixty-year baseball career, whether he fielded winning or losing teams, they never failed to entertain. **IN THIS LETTER TO A FAN, HE SPELLS OUT THE RESPONSIBILITY HE FEELS AN OWNER HAS TO THE FANS.**

CHICAGO WHITE SOX
Dan Ryan at 35th St./Chicago, Ill. 60616/312-924-1000

June 9, 1977

Occupant
4649 Dallas Pl.
Apt. 202
Marlow Heights, MD. 20031

Dear Sir:

     Thank you for your letter and your good wishes.

     I feel that any owner of a major league franchise is obligated to furnish the community an entertaining, interesting ball club and a clean, safe park in which to enjoy the games.

     In return, if the owner fills those requirements, he can expect the community to support his team at the gate.

     If a community does not support a team, and that club fulfills the obligations listed above, then there is no recourse for the owner but to move or sell. By the same token, if the ball club is a poor one, dull, un-interesting and a constant loser, then one cannot blame the fans for staying away from the ball park.

     I hope you do follow through with your plans to visit Comiskey Park and see some of our games. A White Sox schedule is enclosed for you.

     Sincerely yours,

Bill Veeck

BV;ts

enc.

CHARLES NAGY

Born 1967, Bridgeport, Connecticut. A Cleveland Indian his entire career (1990–present), Charles won more games in the American League from 1994 through 1998—73—than all but one pitcher, Mike Mussina. He's a dependable finesse/control-type pitcher who has been a part of the very bad and very good years in Cleveland over the past decade.

I ASKED HIM IF HAVING FRIENDS OR RELATIVES IN THE STANDS EVER MAKES HIM NERVOUS.

It seems like every game you have some relative or friend in the stands watching the game. But when you are out there, they are the furthest thought in your mind. There are times when there are an unusual number, like in the play offs or when you play close to where you grew up, which might make you a little more nervous but like I said after the first pitch the game is all that is on your mind. About being on "center stage" as you put it, just do not look up. Focus on the catcher.

CLEVELAND Indians

Jacobs Field   2401 Ontario Street   Cleveland, OH   44115-4003   www.indian

MONTE PEARSON

Born 1909, Oakland, California.

Died 1978, Fresno, California.

Monte pitched for ten years (1932–1941), mostly with the Cleveland Indians and New York Yankees, compiling a 100–61 won-lost record. He is first on the all-time World Series winning percentage list with a 1.000 winning percentage, having started and won all four games he pitched (in 1936, 1937, 1938, and 1939 for the Yankees). Three of those games were complete games. His 1.01 ERA in World Series play ranks him seventh all-time.

THIS LETTER, WRITTEN BY GENERAL MANAGER BILLY EVANS (AN UMPIRE WHO MADE THE HALL OF FAME IN 1973) TO MONTE EARLY IN MONTE'S CAREER, ILLUSTRATES THAT ELITE ATHLETES WERE NOT IMMUNE TO THE DIFFICULTIES SURROUNDING THE DEPRESSION.

THE CLEVELAND BASEBALL COMPANY

OFFICE AND GROUNDS
LEAGUE PARK
LEXINGTON AT EAST 66TH STREET
CLEVELAND, OHIO

ALVA BRADLEY
Pres.-Treas.

BILLY EVANS
General Manager

W. H. McNICHOLS
Business Manager

R. T. PECKINPAUGH
Manager

January 16 1933

Mr Monte Pearson
3350 Alta Street
Fresno California

Dear Monte Pearson:

During my vacation Mr. Bradley, President of the
Cleveland Baseball Club, sensing the unusual business conditions that
now exist, wrote a letter to all the members of the Cleveland Club, sta
stating very definitely that a curtailment of all salaries would be
necessary for the 1933 season, and asking the players to be guided
accordingly. Since my return, Mr. Bradley has informed me that the
overhead in operating the Cleveland Club must be cut about one-third.
Inasmuch as the matter of players' salaries is the big item, most
of the savings must be made there. I would much prefer to grant you a
raise, rather than give you a cut in salary. However, I am sure you are
familiar with the desperate financial condition that exists in every
business, baseball being no exception.

After five years of operation of a corporation in
which they have put one million dollars, the net results are a matter
of two hundred thousand dollars in the red, taking this into consideration
it is only natural that they should insist on a general curtailment of
all expenses.

Last year you signed a Cleveland contract calling
for $2500.00, and I gave you a bonus of $500.00. This year I am sending
you a contract calling for $3000.00, you being one of the few Cleveland
players whose salary has not been reduced. The figure offered in this
contract is what the owners of the Club, after careful consideration,
feel they can pay.

After you have given these facts careful consideration,
I hope you will reach the conclusion that the salary offered you is not
unfair, and that you will return your contract, signed, at your earliest
convenience.

Very sincerely,

"Billy Evans"

General Manager.

BE-HM
Enc

JIM ROOKER

Born 1942, Lakeview, Oregon. Jim pitched for thirteen years (1968–1980), mostly with the Kansas City Royals and the Pittsburgh Pirates, winning 103 games with a 3.46 ERA. A colorful guy, he went on to become the color commentator for his old team, the Pirates. Jim once said of his former Pirate manager: "Chuck Tanner used to have a bed check just for me every night. No problem. My bed was always there."

I ASKED JIM IF ANYTHING HE SAID ON THE AIR EVER GOT HIM IN TROUBLE.

His journey complete, Rooker celebrates with his family, 1989.

March 6, 1998

Dear Seth:

I want to tell you the story of why I now think before I speak.

I was a color analyst for the Pittsburgh Pirates and we had been on a 7 day road trip in Philadelphia, and up to this point, the trip was a disaster. Little did I know, it was about to get worse! The Pirates had lost all three games in New York, and started off in Philly 0-2. We were then rained out in game 3 which, in my opinion, would have resulted in a win...for the Bucs that is. Finally the torture was almost over. One more game, then home sweet home to the 'Burgh.

Bob Walk started the final game without telling anyone about his sore groin. The good news, however, the Bucs scored 10 runs...yes 10 big ones in their half of the first inning...and boy was this sweet. That's when I commented on the air, "It had been a bad road trip, but if you are going to win just one game, it might as well be the last one. In fact, if we lose this game, I'll walk home."

NEWS BULLETIN...PHILADELPHIA 15   BUCS 11!

The next morning we found ourselves (4 of my buddies joined me) standing on home plate in the Philadelphia Ball Park, where our long journey would begin . Ouch!...what pain. I never imagined how much your feet can hurt when you walk day after day after day. Your feet never get a chance to heel, you just endure the pain.

You might think walking across Pennsylvania through the countryside might be very refreshing. On the contrary. On day number 2, we find ourselves in Lancaster County. Don't get me wrong, it's a nice place, but it was fertilizer season and boy what a smell!

We had many funny experiences along our way such as trying to identify the road kills. We thought maybe we'd open up a restaurant and call it the "Road Kill Cafe" with the slogan "Fresh from the road to your plate!"

As I said, 13 days and 320 miles of painful but worthwhile days later, we finally entered the Hill District in Pittsburgh. Both sides of the street were crammed with well wishers saying things like, "great going", and "way to go Rook, you kept your word." We raised $81,000 for charity. There is, however, one lesson I learned : I am now very careful about the things I say.

NOTE: Philly to Pittsburgh was bad, but thank god we weren't playing against San Francisco!

Jim Rooker

Leon Cadore

Joe Oesehger

ZACK WHEAT

Born 1888, Hamilton, Missouri. Died 1972, Sedalia, Missouri. Zack was the most beloved Brooklyn Robins player when he played right field for them from 1909 to 1926, hitting .317. He was a participant on May 1, 1920, in a twenty-six-inning, 1–1 tie game—the longest major-league game ever to end deadlocked. The duel pitted the Robins' Leon Cadore against the Boston Braves' Joe Oeschger. They both pitched the entire game. Cadore faced ninety-five hitters, Oeschger eighty-five. (The average pitcher today faces thirty-eight hitters per game.) Oeschger almost won the game for himself by hitting what appeared to be a home run in the ninth inning, but Wheat made a spectacular catch to keep the game going for what turned out to be another seventeen innings. The next day, Brooklyn played a thirteen-inning game against the Phillies which they lost, 4–3. The day after that, they played a nineteen-inning game against the Braves, losing again, 2–1. In the fifty-eight innings Brooklyn played over those three days, they did not use one relief pitcher. Seven weeks later Brooklyn played the Braves in a replay of their twenty-six-inning affair. They lost 1–0 to . . . Joe Oeschger.

IN A LETTER TO A FRIEND IN 1970 ZACK REMEMBERED THE CIRCUMSTANCES SURROUNDING THE AMAZING TWENTY-SIX-INNING TIE GAME.

The 26 inn. game — it was quite a game — there was quite a few good plays that kept the score down — also good pitching by both Cadore and Oeschger — If I remember right we jumped out of Boston that nite & played 17 inn in Brooklyn the next day (Sun) went to Boston that nite & played there Mon. 19 inn. We lost both of those games — but that same year (1920) we won the pennant. I doubt if that game will ever be beat — but, records are to be broken & that one may beaten.

My best regards —
Sincerely
Zack D. Wheat,

MARIUS RUSSO

Born 1914, Brooklyn, New York. Marius pitched from 1939 until 1946 with the New York Yankees, winning 45 and losing 34, with a 3.13 ERA. He also had two complete-game World Series victories (1941, 1943). Less than a month into his pitching career, he was on the Yankee Stadium field, July 4, 1939, when his stricken teammate, Lou Gehrig, delivered a speech that is often referred to as the Gettysburg Address of baseball.

I ASKED HIM HIS RECOL- LECTION OF THE MOST EMOTIONAL AFTERNOON IN THE GAME'S HISTORY.

AUG. 16, 1997

Dear Seth —

YES, I REMEMBER LOU GEHRIG'S SPEECH THAT AFTERNOON VERY WELL. LOU DID AN EXCELLENT JOB AT THE MIKE — HIS SPEECH WAS HEART-RENDERING. ALL WAS STILL, NOT A SOUND ANYWHERE. BOTH TEAMS DIDN'T MISS A WORD. THERE WERE MANY TEARS. I REMEMBER ESPECIALLY TONY LAZZERI. ALSO MURPHY & GOMEZ — LOU'S TEAMMATES FOR MANY YEARS, CRYING UNABASHEDLY.

WHEN BABE RUTH EMBRACED GEHRIG, IT MADE EVERYONE HAPPY & MANY SMILES SHOWED THROUGH WET EYES. THE TWO GREAT BALL-PLAYERS. THE GREATEST IN OUR TIME.

YES, SETH, I REMEMBER THAT DAY WELL. MY ROOKIE SEASON — AND I MET SO MANY GOOD PLAYERS. ALL THE BEST

YOURS

Marius Russo

N.Y. YANKEES

1939-'43, '46

TOMMY HENRICH

Born 1913, Massillon, Ohio. A speedy outfielder, "Old Reliable" was one of the great Yankees of the 1930s and 1940s. He earned his nickname with his continuous supply of clutch hits. He was a solid career .282 hitter who led the league in triples in 1948 (13) and 1949 (14). When Brooklyn Dodgers catcher Mickey Owen dropped the strike that would have given the Dodgers a victory in the crucial fourth game of the 1941 World Series, Henrich was the batter. (Henrich said that Dodger Hugh Casey's pitch fooled him so badly that he thought it might have a chance to fool catcher Owen, which it did!) The Yankee teams Tommy played on from 1937 to 1950 won eight pennants and six world championships. His first two years in the majors were his teammate Lou Gehrig's last two full years in baseball. **I ASKED HIM IF LOU GAVE HIM ANY ADVICE ON PITCHERS HE WAS TO FACE FOR THE FIRST TIME, AND ALSO WHAT KIND OF GUY GEHRIG WAS.**

"What a belter he was..." Lou loses one, 1926.

Seth

I am very honored to have been
a good friend of Lou Gehrig.

He was extremely generous in giving me
all the advice I asked for regarding pitchers
I was to face for the first time.

He kidded me quite a bit. I felt
very close to him because of it.

I played only the last two years
with him but that was long enough
for me to recognize what a better he was.

He was a kind man but when he
swung a bat he looked like he was
swinging a tomahawk ready to kill the
ball no matter where the pitcher threw it.

Bill Dickey & Lou were always together
& I'm glad to say they were two of the
greatest guys I ever met.

Sincerely
Tom

"Old Reliable's" old reliables

The entire text of Lou Gehrig's speech, July 4, 1939:

Fans, for the past two weeks you have been reading about the bad break I got. Yet today I consider myself the luckiest man on the face of the earth. I have been in ballparks for seventeen years and have never received anything but kindness and encouragement from you fans. Look at these grand men. Which of you wouldn't consider it the highlight of his career just to associate with them for even one day? Sure, I'm lucky. Who wouldn't consider it an honor to have known Jacob Ruppert? Also, the builder of baseball's greatest empire, Ed Barrow? To have spent six years with that wonderful little fellow, Miller Huggins? Then to have spent the next nine years with that outstanding leader, that smart student of psychology, the best manager in baseball today, Joe McCarthy? Sure I'm lucky. When the New York Giants, a team you would give your right arm to beat, and vice versa, sends you a gift-- that's something. When everybody down to the groundskeepers and those boys in the white coats remember you with trophies--that's something. When you have a wonderful mother-in-law who takes sides with you in squabbles with her own daughter--that's something. When you have a father and a mother who work all their lives so you can have an education and build your body-- it's a blessing. When you have a wife who has been a tower of strength and shown more courage than you dreamed existed--that's the finest I know. So I close in saying that I may have had a tough break, but I have an awful lot to live for. Thank you.

May 9 1998

Seth:

The first part to your question about feeling alone is true. The mound is an 18 foot circle which I consider is my office. In my office my objective is to work together with my catcher through signs and both of our senses working together in sinc. My objective is to throw strikes, work fast, and utilize my defense. I do feel alone because ultimately I have the final say in what pitch is thrown. Which does have an effect on the outcome of the game. So it is important because my teamates, fans, and myself have high expectations, of myself.

A pitcher has many thoughts while on the mound. Some of which can be fear, domination, intimidation, situations, counts, base-runners location of pitches, memory of pitches thrown previously, how a hitter has had success or failure off of you, on deck hitter, tempo of oneself, and finally just getting hitters out! I feel the biggest thought is to stay positive with your thoughts and be aggressive. It doesn't matter whether you are a power pitcher or finess pitcher. The object is to get the hitter out and allow your team to hit to score runs.

Jamie Moyer

VIOLET WHITEHILL GEISSINGER

Born 1901, San Jose, California. Violet Oliver was a California model who is best known as the face on the Sun-Maid raisin box. She was hanging out with baseball players in the 1920s when she met her future husband, Detroit Tiger pitcher Earl Whitehill, who many considered, along with pitcher Wes Ferrell, the best-looking baseball player of his era. Earl was a starting pitcher from 1923 to 1939 with the Detroit Tigers (1923–1932), Washington Senators (1933–1936), Cleveland Indians (1937–1938), and Chicago Cubs (1939). He won 218 games, including the third game of the 1933 World Series with a complete game, six-hit shutout against the New York Giants. **I ASKED VIOLET ABOUT EARL'S COURTSHIP OF HER.**

Dear Seth:—

It was the end of the 1925 Base Ball Season and everyone was going home for the winter months. A good friend on the Detroit team, Harry Hielman, insisted I meet his friend Earl Whitehill. He knew I would like him. Harry Hielman was also a good friend of Babe Ruth & his wife Claire. So Mrs. Ruth gave a lovely dinner party and Harry Hielman brought Earl along. So we met!

When I was in New York I always stayed with Claire and her mother and two brothers. This was before she and Babe married.

Yes, Earl Whitehill was a handsome man and I liked him very much. We all had a fun time that night.
He wanted to know if I ever thought of getting married? Later I told him "yes" I'll marry you Earl.*

We had twenty seven years of marriage.

Thank you again Seth, just for being you.
—Violet

JEAN FAUT

Born 1925, East
Greenville, Pennsylvania.
Jean was the greatest
pitcher in the All-American
Girls Professional Baseball
League, the league depict-
ed in the popular movie *A
League of Their Own*.
She pitched for the South
Bend Blue Sox, compiling
a 140–64 won-lost
record with an amazing
1.23 earned run average.
Jean had two perfect
games and was named
Player of the Year in 1951
and 1953. **I ASKED
HER HOW SHE HAPPENED
TO BECOME A PITCHER.**

Dear Seth,

My favorite pastime growing up in a small town which was fortunate to host a semi-pro baseball team was practicing with that team every evening. A few of those players taught me all the pitches. I pitched an exhibition game with them, or I should say I made an appearance.

When the All American Girls Professional Baseball League (AAGPBL) switched from underhanded pitching to overhand, I was 'home free'. I developed my excellent control by throwing stones a long distance at telephone poles by the hour in the alley behind my home. Never realizing how valuable that experience would be a few years later.

The eight years I played in the AAGPBL were the most memorable years of my life. To <u>follow your dream</u> is the greatest accomplishment you can experience.

Sincerely,
Jean

BILL VOISELLE

Born 1919, Greenwood, South Carolina. Bill pitched for nine years (1942–1950) with four teams, including the pennant-winning Boston Braves in 1948. That year's famous line was "Spahn and Sain and pray for rain." Bill, as the third starter that year did not warrant the "pray for rain" status to which he was relegated, gaining 13 victories. A native of a town named Ninety-Six, South Carolina, he proudly wore the number on his Braves uniform, the highest number worn by a player up to that point. **I ASKED HIM WHETHER THE TOWN EVER SHOWED ITS APPRECIATION TO HIM.**

On 9/6/96 the Town of "96" honored 'ole 96. A picture of 'ole 96 hangs in the town welcoming center. Yes, this town has honored me.

The jersey I kept until a few years ago, sold it to a big Atlanta fan.

Bill Voiselle

LARRY YOUNT

Born 1950, Houston, Texas. The older brother of Hall of Fame short-stop/center fielder Robin Yount, Larry's lifelong dream was to pitch for the Houston Astros. He was called up from the minors by them in 1971, his wish on the verge of being fulfilled. On his very first warm-up toss, while on the mound for his professional pitching debut with his dream team, he injured his right shoulder and could not throw a single pitch. He was sent back down to the minors, his career over.

I WONDERED IF HE EVER THINKS BACK ON THAT DAY AND ASKS HIMSELF "WHAT IF?"

I know you had to dig deep to find out about me, so I'll get the story right for you, & then a couple of thoughts.

I was called up in late 1971 from the minors and was called into the game to pitch. Being 21, I knew before going to the mound that my elbow was in pain, but figured that the excitement of the moment would make the pain go away. Warming up on the mound I actually used good judgement and pulled myself before I really got hurt. The following year after a great spring training I was sent to the minors, never to return to the major leagues.

THOUGHTS

1 - If I ever thought that would be my only opportunity to pitch in the major leagues, I would have done so.

2 I would have faced Henry Aaron

3 To this day I can't believe I was not a successful pitcher in the major leagues.

4 I was able to accomplish about a 120% of my business ability and only 80% of my athletic ability.

5 I now have a great family and could not be much happier, except that void of not accomplishing my boyhood dreams.

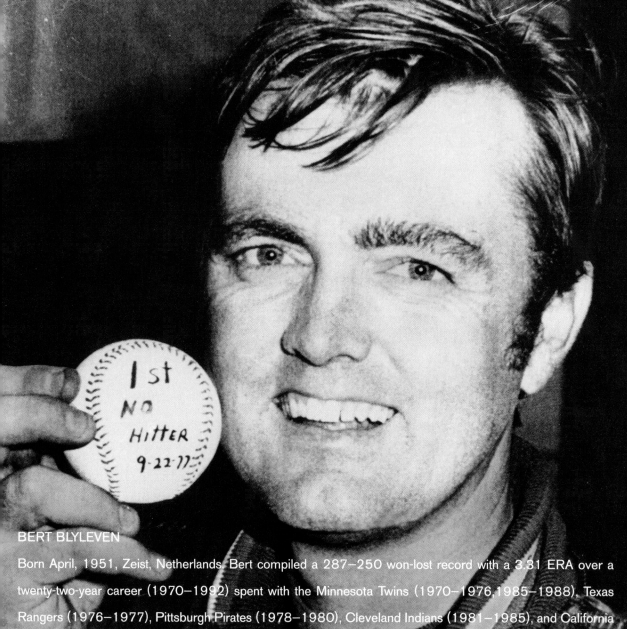

BERT BLYLEVEN

Born April, 1951, Zeist, Netherlands. Bert compiled a 287–250 won-lost record with a 3.31 ERA over a twenty-two-year career (1970–1992) spent with the Minnesota Twins (1970–1976,1985–1988), Texas Rangers (1976–1977), Pittsburgh Pirates (1978–1980), Cleveland Indians (1981–1985), and California Angels (1989–1990, 1992). An off-speed-pitch specialist, Bert struck out more hitters in his career— 3,701—than anyone except Nolan Ryan and Steve Carlton. His sixty career shutouts rank tenth all-time.

I ASKED HIM IF AFTER TWENTY YEARS ON THE MOUND IT WAS HARD TO RETIRE.

MINNESOTA TWINS

Western Division Champions: 1969, 1970, 1987, 1991
American League Champions: 1965, 1987, 1991
World Champions: 1987, 1991

Media Relations Department: (612) 375-74

Dear Seth,

Wish I could have pitched until I die

Good luck in life,

Bert

185

WAITE HOYT

Born 1899, Brooklyn, New York. Died 1984,
Cincinnati, Ohio. He won 237 games in a
career (1918–1938) most notably spent
with the powerful New York Yankees of the
1920s. Besides being a Hall of Fame
pitcher (inducted in 1969), Waite was
an eloquent speaker, a painter and a
professional singer, appearing in a
vaudeville act with Jimmy
Durante. As the announcer for
the Reds from 1942 to
1966, he was known for the
vivid stories he would recol-
lect during long rain
delays.

**WAITE REMEMBERS A
TIME GONE BY.**

WAITE C. HOYT
2444 MADISON ROAD
CINCINNATI, OHIO 45208

March 7th, 1978

Dear Friend,

It is snowing once again--plus a
little sleet--all of which I suppose is nothing
compared to the rain and floods in California.

I surely appreciated that nice letter==and I too
lok back upon the thirties (and the twenties) with
deep nostalhia. The game, the personnel, the rules,
equipment, the very phjlosophy has changed so much, I
cannot view baseball today as I once did. I live ,
and am well acquainted in this city which boasts of
the Reds. The owners of the Reds the management, are
all friends of mine, thus I have a real interest in
their success--but what I do not say, it seems to me
the actual sport is no longer. The dreamy afternoons
for the bleacherites--the practices and life style of
the players,all gone--the advancing world has
cancelled all that along w th the old swimmin' hole,
and the long-branch fishin' pole.

So letters like yours have meaning and I am
grateful for your time and effort--and sentiments.
Ebbets Field--gone. Polo Grounds gone. Yankee
Stadium renovated--you can have it. A spice of life,
natural and unsullied--the young of today will never
know, much less experience.

I'm sorry that I have no pictures. They faded
and cracked to pieces long ago.

Sincerely

Waite C. Hoyt.

187

TRANSCRIPTS

Carl Pavano

Seth,

In response to your letter, I am going to answer the question so many have asked. I knew it was the last game of the season and of my rookie year with the Montreal Expos. While sitting on the bench the previous three games against the Cardinals, I said to myself 'all along' if I get a chance to pitch against McGuire, I will *not* walk him. I will *challenge* and *beat* him.

First time in my professional career going into a game as a relief pitcher, he steps in as I tow the rubber. A 3 to 3 tie with 2 outs in the bottom of the eigth with 2 men on. 52,000 people up on their feet cheering. First pitch, CRACK—GONE, #70

And the rest is History

Carl Pavano

Steve Carlton

Dear Seth:

My decision not to speak to the media was not the result of any one incident. The media was crossing lines that had been drawn in baseball for many years. Reporting on the personal lives of players and breaking the trust that came with their access to the players. I felt it would be better for me and the fans if they covered me from the press box.

Looking back, I think that the writing was better and definitely more creative after I stopped speaking to the media.

Thanks for asking

Steve Carlton

Kerry Wood

12/3/98

Seth,

The day after I struck out 20, I got a call from Roger. At first, when I was told he was on the phone I thought it was a joke. And when I picked up the phone he said, "Hey Kerry this is Rocket, congratulations." I didn't know what to say. I had never met Roger, just talked a couple of times on the phone. But still I was a little nervous. He just said that he was happy for me and proud to be sharing the record with me. I met Roger for the first time in Orlando, at the Players Choice Awards. He is a great person, has a wonderful family, and it was a honor to meet him. It's something I will never forget.

Sincerely,

Kerry Wood

Roger Clemens

(see p. 11 for typewritten letter)

Cy Young

Dear Sir—

One way to learn this game is to take lots of time. Play ball as often as you can—Pick out some spot you like in the game—that was the way I done. Then get a chance for a try out. After you are serious you can make the grade.

Do not think you can learn it overnight. You can learn after 13 yrs—20 yrs. At least i learned till the end of my career

Yours

Cy Young

Gary Kroll

Seth,

August 15, 1965, Shea, the Beatles

I was there, got to meet the Beatles. The atmosphere at the park that night was electrical hysteria, or better put a magical happening. It was the 60s, it was new york, it was the Beatles. A one time experience.

Gary Kroll

Mace Brown

Seth:

After "Babe" Ruth hit his 3rd homer of the game, which cleared the roof of the double deck stand, he crossed home plate, and he ran directly into our dug out and sat right beside me on the end of the bench. He sat there for about 4 or 5 minutes, right next to me. The only thing I remember him saying was, "Boy's that last one felt good."

Sincerly,

Mace Brown

Al Hrabosky

Mr. Swirsky

I developed my self psyche technique solely as a motivation for myself. This enabled me to have my "controled hate mood" to destroy each batter. At the same time it took some hitters out of their mental approach to the game. Guys that would never step out of the batters box were stepping out trying to out psyche the master. They would try to out think me. As a result, I would be able to throw a pitch when their minds weren't completely focused on hitting. I have to much respect for my competitors to ever think that I 'owned' anyone.

As to Mr. Vern Rapp and his 'no facial hair': No, I don't think Vern understood what my long hair and Fu Manchu meant to my psyche on the mound. Vern did not institute the rule to punish me, but as a result the Mad Hungarian felt like a soldier going to war without his rifle! Psyche up!

Al Hrabosky

The Mad Hungarian

Turk Wendell

"Got on the Throne"

During the 1996 season, as I played for the Chicago Cubs, I got into a daily routine. This went from the time I got to the ballpark, right up to throwing my warm-ups to go into the game.

The routine was that I always used the restrooms during the fifth inning.

We were playing the L.A. Dodgers in L.A., and it was a day game. That meant we occupied the right field grandstands. Well, when the fifth inning rolled around I informed all my bullpen mates and coach Dave Bialas that I'd be in the bathroom. They all acknowledged where I'd be as I departed.

There I sat on the "'Ol mighty Poursalin(sp?) God" when Dave open the door the bullpen restroom wide open! Everyone in the grandstand laughed, and started waving to me. Well, being literally caught with my pants down, I could do nothing but wave back.

Dave apologized up and down and shut the door and quickly as he could, but the damage was done!

When I was done I opened the door and the crowd roared, laughed, and waved again! What an embarassment!

Turk Wendell

Jeff Bagwell

Seth,

Pitchers, as a group, are generally strange. They have different opinions of the game than the every day to day players.

Starting pitchers spend 4 days not paying attention to the game, and on the 5th day, their start, they have no idea whats going on. You generally find the best pitchers in the game pay attention more consistently than others.

Relief pitchers are more in tune with situations in the game because their roles are more similar to the every day player.

Despite an every day players perspective, the game couldn't be played without pitchers.

Sincerly,

Jeff Bagwell

Curt Schilling

(see p. 25 for typewritten letter)

Warren Buffett

(see p. 27 for typewritten letter)

Chan Ho Park

(see p. 29 for typewritten letter)

Les Mueller

12-2-97

Dear Seth,

I did admire Pete Gray as I am sure most players did. He played very well considering the handicap and I was not shocked that he got a hit—But let me tell you I really was shocked when he just missed by a few feet of hitting a home run off me in another game. I came in relief late in the game with several men on base and he put our right fielder in Detroit up against the wall and just gave me a save in that game, so I almost gave him his first and only homer in the Big League's Ha!

Best Wishes,

Les Mueller

Jerry Reuss

Seth, 6/20/97

Same players . . . Different wives

Jerry Reuss

Ken Krahenbuhl

Having to explain to friends and family that you were traded for fish is the most humiliating thing I had ever done

Throwing a perfect game the next day was the most satisfying.

In my 8yr minor league career I never thought being traded for catfish would bring me so much attention, but it has. A perfect game is a great milestone in any pitchers career but it was 10 pounds of catfish that brought me fame. All the attention has giving me many oppertunity's I may have never gotten especially to a guy who has had 4 elbow surgerys. Baseball is truely a funny game

Ken Krahenbuhl

"Catfish"

Rocky Colavito

8-21-97

Dear Seth,

To answer your question, Shock! Total shock. I was told while I was the baserunner at first base in the last spring training game traveling north, in Memphis, Tennessee. Joe Gordon approached me and said 'Rocky thats the last time you will bat as a Cleveland Indian, you've been traded to the Detroit Tigers for Harvey Kuenn.' I saw Frank Love many times after the trade. I cant think of anything nice to say about him so I wont say anything at all.

Sincerely,

Rocky Colavito

P.S. Gordon was wrong!

Pete Harnisch

12/11/98

I don't know if it made me a better pitcher, but I do know that it put less importance on the outcome of games. Perspective is a wonderful thing. Being away when I was sick did two things;

1. Re-emphasized the importance of family and real friends! 2. Put into perspective the importance of baseball in my life. (It's a small percentage but sometimes that gets lost when you're pitching poorly!)

To summarize, my being away from the game put the game into perspective. If you work very hard to be in excellent physical shape and be prepared to pitch than it's all you can do. Give 100% and accept the results. A valuable lesson I'm just now starting to learn!!!

Pete Harnisch

Justin Thompson

Seth

It's a honor to be named a #1 starter. A lot of expectations come with the role because your team expects you to go out there every five days and give them a strong performance. The way I look at the situation is that it's a great challenge because you always face other teams #1 starters which means lots of times your not going to get the run support. So when you get a couple of runs you really got to bear down and show them why you are a #1 starter. It definitely is one of the most challenging tasks that I have every tried but I also wouldn't change it for the world.

Justin Thompson

Carl Mays

Wensday - 28th

Ive had to live with this thing with hitting Chatman. The papers said I was guilty and the general public believes everything they see in the paper.

Chatman was hit because when he shifted his back foot we all knew he was going to push the ball down the first base line, if he did no one could throw him out, he was so fast, so we would bring the ball up, to try to make him pop it up, so he ran into a high pitch, over the plate— Please make a mental picture of this for me. it would be my first and last request—the the umpire said in all the paperes, "the ball was over the plate high"—Huggins fined me. Every word of this is true.

Ive never been very lucky, and I blame the most of it on lack of education, which I wanted more than anything, but it was denied me, no Father, no money, Country school, and had to stay home to help feed the family.

Lots of Love

Carl

Don Newcombe

Dear Seth,

We have come a long way in race relations since Jackie Robinson, Roy Campanella, Larry Doby and myself first came on the baseball scene, however there still is a long way to go. For example: We all can live and eat with our teammates now, but in my era that wasn't possible in some of our American cities, and I've always asked Why? We could fight and die for our country when necessary, but we could'nt stay at the same hotel. We could pay our taxes if we had a job of some sort, but we couldn't play baseball except when you were separated. Jackie Robinson helped to change all that, but a white man had to give him a chance first. So, I'll be forever indebted to Branch Rickey for my chance, but Jackie Robinson was the inspiration that young kids as I need to succeed in our country today and now that chance is available to them. So Yes, we've come a long way in all this, but the struggle, and it was a struggle is far from over, overall.

As ever

Don Newcombe

David Cone

12-4-98

Dear Seth—

Are we the greatest team of all time? How does one make comparisons that span decade upon decade?

After losing three out of our first four games, the 1998 New York Yankees went 149-46 to finish with a 125-50 [124–47] record of historical proportions. The numbers are staggering but the attitude and professionalism of the Yanks are even more impressive. There were major contributions from all corners of the clubhouse that help create an atmosphere of selflessness and depth the likes of which are arguably unparalleled in the history of baseball. This team gave new meaning to the old cliché, "The sum is greater than it's parts." Not one player stood head and shoulders above any other. From pitching and defense, to speed and power, all of the bases were literally covered. One must also consider a team that displayed incredible heart and character that evolved from some of the most compelling human interest stories ever witnessed and covered in New York sports history.

I say it's an honor for us to be mentioned in that context and I hope the great debate goes on and on and on. It seems to me that this is how legends and legendary teams are made.

Sincerely—

David Cone '98 Yanks

Walter "Dutch" Ruether

In the 1st place dont try to compare any of the modern day ball club to the 927 Yankees—There is no comparison. The 27 Yankee would win either pennant National or American league by at least 30 games.

Babe Ruth had to be the most valuable player on any club.

The most underated player I would say was Mark Koenig.

My contribution was 13 games won and 6 lost by the 1st of August. I did not pitch another inning all year on account of a suit I had filed against the Hearst publications.

Hope this helps a little.

Walter "Dutch" Ruether

Elias Sosa

I felt butterflies in my stomach facing R.J. in the 1977 World Series as I ran from the bullpen to the pitching mound, knowing that Yankee Stadium was Jampacked.

The scouting report on R.J. was to stay hard up and in with a good fast-ball. I dont have any regrets about that pitch. My catcher Steve Yeager came to the mound and said, "he hit a very good pitch."

Whether he was guessing or not, I have to give him credit. I went out and did exactly what I was sup-posed to do. Even though the result was negative.

Elias Sosa

Reggie Jackson

(see p. 49 for typewritten letter)

Jim Palmer

October 25, 1998

Dear Seth,

A moment I am fond of happened in the mid seventies in a game I pitched against the Texas Rangers. I had a 102-degree temperature and there was some question whether I would be able to pitch. I did and after retiring the Rangers in order in the 1st inning, the Orioles scored 5 runs in the bottom of the first. I was sitting next to Earl Weaver and he looked at me and remarked, "I know you don't feel well, but imagine how sick you would feel if you were home in bed and we scored 5 runs in the 1st." We both laughed and for one of the few times, I had to agree with Earl.

Jim Palmer

Whit Wyatt

(see p. 54 for typewritten letter)

Vic Raschi

October 3, 1979

Casey Stengel was a very nice person and human being.

He helped all of his players and treated them as humans.

He was the most knowledgeable manger that I knew.

He was always ahead of everyone else in decision making.

great guy.

Best wishes

Vic Raschi

Terry Collins

12/4/97

Dear Seth,

Thanks for your letter. In reference to your question, No! Never has a pitcher refused to give me the ball. Many have tried to talk their way into staying in the game and some have succeeded. But when I make my decision to take them out it is over!

I don't think pitchers resent coming out of a game but many do not want or like to come out. Some can't wait to get out!

Thanks for writing.

All the best

Terry Collins

Mike Krukow

(see p. 57 for typewritten letter)

Richard Nixon

(see p. 59 for typewritten letter)

Anne Pitcher Brosnan

(see p. 61 for typewritten letter)

Bill Lee

Seth

As you can see my free hand sucks. If you want the real story—one thing I remember before Perez Zimmer Moved Doyle out of double play position! Check out full replay of game.

Bill Lee

Tom Glavine

Dear Seth,

Competition is what drives me—Competition between me and the hitter trying to be better than him. Also, the competition with myself trying to get better year in and year out and not setteling for where I am and the success I've had—the competition makes the game so much fun, and believe me, it really is a great way to make a living!

Sincerely

Tom Glavine

Dickie Kerr

Sept-11-1938

Friend

I am trying to line up a job for 1939 in base ball.

Do not care what kind, whether as manager, coach or scout, so am writing you to find out if you can place me somewhere.

See where Hot Springs will be your farm next year, would like to go there and develop some ball players for you.

May I hear from you soon?

With kindest regards, I am

Dick Kerr

124 E. Cherry-St.

"Shoeless Joe" Jackson

Dear Mr. Jackson

I am in the 8th Grade and am 13 yrs. old My father talks about you very much. He considers you the best ballplayer ever lived second only to the great Ty Cobb. I play left field on my school team. My hobby is base-ball. I read about you in books. Will you please send me your autograph. I have enclosed an envelope with my name and address on it and a piece of paper for you to sign on. Thank you very much.

Sincerely yours,

William Bennethum

432 north 10th St.

Reading, Pennsylvania

Judge Kenesaw Mountain Landis

(see p. 75 for typewritten letter)

Bob Friend

(see p. 77 for typewritten letter)

Fay Vincent

(see p. 78 for typewritten letter)

Dave Campbell

11/28/97

Seth,

I'd say the biggest difference watching baseball in the late 1990's compared to playing in the late 60's and early 70's was the depth of quality starting pitching. In the National League, almost every team had at least two quality starters and many had three or four. There weren't too many soft touches. They also went deeper into the game so one didn't get to face a lot of watered down mid-relief pitching so prevelent today.

Guys like Curt Shilling and Roger Clemens are throwbacks to another era. Power, power, and more power. I'd compare Shilling to Denny Mc Lain's years of 1968 and 1969 and Clemens to Tom Seaver.

Luis Tiant in his prime would compare favorably to Pedro Martinez, but it's tough to compare Greg Maddux to anyone from the era as he's so unique. Pedro also would compare to Bob Gibson because they both had a mean streak.

It's also tougher to pitch today because of a much smaller strike zone, especially in the American League.

Good Luck

Dave Campbell

Luis Tiant

Dear Seth

My most satisfying moment in baseball was my 1st game in the big leages agains the Yankees,

I won 3–0 and struck out 11. Also tied a record by striking out 11 in my 1st M.L start.

I got my original delivery by showing my number to the batter. I started this in Boston. I then started to look at the clouds and the people. And since it work I kept doing it.

Luis Tiant

Chet Hoff

I hoped for a great game. It was the 1st game I ever played with the Yankees and surprisingly enough I ended up pitching to Ty Cobb. I remember striking out Ty Cobb that day—He was the only batter that could hit 400—a great guy—

Chet Hoff

Jaret Wright

I had spoke to my dad just a little before the game and he said to enjoy what was going on and to have confidence in myself. After the game he said that I should be proud of what the team and myself had done.

Jaret Wright

Clyde Wright

Nov 28, 1998

Seth,

Yes, it was hard to watch my son pitch the seventh game. It was twice as hard for my wife to watch! Every parent wants' their kids to do well. It doesn't matter what field. Jaret just happened to be on National T.V. with millions of people watching. The one thing that calmed me down was big Jack Nicklaus was their. I kept telling myself "he came to see my son pitch!" Yes, I know he is from Florida, wishful thinking!

Clyde Wright

By the time Jaret was a junior in H.S. I knew he had a good chance to play pro-ball.

Hub Kittle

(see p. 89 for typewritten letter)

John "Blue Moon" Odom

Dear Seth,

My nickname "Blue Moon" was given to me in the fifth grade, by a classmate by the name of Joe Morris. It first started out by him using the name "Moon Head" and shortly after went to "Blue Moon".

Ever since that has been my nickname. Alot of people believe that Charles O. Finley the former Oakland A's owner gave me the "Nickname." He did name a few of the player's such as "Catfish"

In the beginning; I did not like it; after a while I got used to it and ever since it has stuck!

John "Blue Moon" Odom

Oakland A's #13

Barry Halper

(see p. 93 for typewritten letter)

Walter Johnson

(see p. 95 for typewritten letter)

Mel Harder

9/16/97

Dear Seth:

I pitched for Walter Johnson in 1933, 34 and 35 and they were the best years of my career.

Walter was a high class, Gentleman, type person and easy man to work for.

Muddy Ruel, who caught Walter at Washington and later a coach for Cleveland tells how Walter, who had the best fast ball in Baseball, would shake-off 'Muddy's' fast ball sign, so he could throw his little curve ball. Walter was proud of his curve, but 'Muddy' would always make him throw his fast ball. I believe Walter Johnson was the greatest pitcher of all time.

Best Regards,

Mel Harder

Bill Wambsganss

The greatest pitcher that I ever saw and batted against was Walter Johnson.

The greatest hitter was Babe Ruth. There was also Ty Cobb. Ruth was also a *very* good left-handed pitcher I batted against him too.

Wamby

C. J. Nitkowski

(see p. 111 for typewritten letter)

Mike Torrez

Dear Seth,

The 1978 Yankees/Red Sox playoff game was truly a memorable moment in baseball, especially for me as the losing pitcher of record.

I really don't think about it unless it is mentioned (which is quite often) or highlighted on Classic Sport Network.

For me this is positive, as it has kept my name in baseball, via newspapers and T.V. People tend to forget my great "77" playoff and 2-World Series games wins for the Yanks! When Bucky Dent's new stadium opened in Florida, we re-enacted that all too familiar pitch. It took him 20 swings just to hit it out of the "Little Green Monster" in Florida. Even today we see each other several times a year.

I kid him alot about using a cork bat (Mickey Rivers bat). I will tell you this, all those Yankees used to cork (Ha-Ha).

Take Care

Mike Torrez

Jose Lima

It doesn't feel good because i already gave up #50 and 51 back in Chicago and everybody said that i grooved it to him. I know in my heart I didn't and thats all that matters to me.

When Sammy hit #66, I was mad at myself because I don't want people to say the same thing again. When I faced McGuire I challenged him. I pitched the same way I do to everybody. No one scares me. Ive been pitching like that all my life.

No two people are more deserving of breaking the record than Mark McGuire and Sammy Sosa . . Jose Lima

Robin Roberts

Seth—

The home runs that decided a game caused much anguish—If the home run didn't alter the score it was just another run—

I had both kinds—Too many in fact! Sorry you mentioned it.

Sincerely

Robin Roberts

Stu Miller

Mantle hit a 3 and 2 pitch that was a little low and a little outside—ball four—it was my best pitch a straight change-up. He had to be looking for it. I tip my hat to him—a great hitter.

It was the only home run he hit off me in my five years with the Orioles.

Stu Miller

Art Ditmar

Dear Seth,

In regard to the law suit I had with Anheiser-Busch beer regarding their bogus commercial back in 1985 was eventually thrown out of court but did reach the Supreme Court.

The judge in Cleveland felt that throwing a home run ball was 'not that big a deal' so she threw the case out.

I still feel that no company has a right to misuse your name in a situation they knew was incorrect.

Thank you for your interest.

Art Ditmar

Balor Moore

3/09/98

I remember Mike Schmidt's 1st home run very well. The story goes like this: I was a 21 yr old rookie in '72 and had been pitching very well at the time. My previous 2 starts had been shutouts against the Mets and the Pirates plus a few more innings against the Braves. We were leading the Phillies going into the bottom of the 8th by 1−0. Philly had loaded the bases with no outs. I remember thinking about the situation but pitching as well as I had been at the time I thought I still could escape the inning. The 4th hitter of the inning hit a liner to Foli at short who dove to his left making the catch and flipping to 2nd for a double play, the runner at 3rd holding. Now we have 1st and 3rd, 2 outs and a pinch hitter is announced. I look at the scoreboard and see it is a guy named Schmidt, just called up from the minors. The catcher, I remember it being Bocabella but Tim McCarver remembers catching that game, comes to the mound and ask what I know about Schmidt? We decide not to get beat on anything but my fastball. After 2 pitches we have the count in our favor 0 and 2 and call for a fastball low and away. Good call, bad pitch. Normally my fastball away will tail off the plate but in this instance it started low and away and ran back over the heart of the plate. As I faced Schmidt many more times this was a pitch I found he could hit and hit very far, which he did that Sept. nite at the Vet. On that pitch the Phillies went on to win 3−2, my consecutive scoreless streak ended at 27+ innings and Mike Schmidt hit his 1st big league home run.

Balor Moore

Jim Bouton

(see p. 121 for typewritten letter)

Don Liddle

Seth,

The situation in the First game of the World Series, was a relief pitcher's nightmare. Men on first and second and nobody out. Fredie Fitzsimons was the one who was on the mound waving me into the ball game. When I arrived at the mound he asked me if I remember how they wanted Wertz pitched, I answered yes, hes a good low ball hitter. With nobody out West Westrum our catcher told me, he may bunt, as there was nobody out.

The first pitch was a high inside fast ball, he looked at it high, for a ball. Now we threw him another fast ball up, but we wanted it away, we caught the outside corner for a strike, now Wes said he'll bunt now. We came back high and tight, he bunted the ball toward the Cleveland dugout. Too good of a hitter to bunt with two strikes so we showed him a curve outside for a ball, came back with a fast ball away and up, he hit it deep to center field.

After the game in the Club House, I lockered next to Willie and when Leo Durocher came over the congratulate Willie on "the Catch," I told Leo well, 'I got my man,' just to belittle the great catch Willie made.
Don Liddle

Rolando Arrojo

(see p. 124 for typewritten letter)

Max Lanier

Dec. 30, 1996
Dear Mr. Swirsky,
I couldn't believe baseball conditions could be so different until I got to Mexico. They had wonderful fans but terrible fields. We had a railroad track between the outfield and infield and when the train went through they had to open the gates for it to go through.

It was really hard to throw a curve ball in Mexico City and Puebla because of the high altitude.

In 1946 it was election time in Mexico and "Aliman" was running for president and he was the owner "George Pasquel's" bro. law. That is the reason "Pasquel" got us, the fans love baseball & they voted for "Aliman."

Even our clubhouse Man said he voted seven times.
Sincerely,
Max Lanier

Al Pratt

From my earliest recollection I had a ball. In 1858 I played my first base-ball and cricket with the boys on the commons of Allegheny and played until July 14, 1864. My base-ball career being cut short by enlisting in the Civil War in the one hundred day service with Captain James Crow—Company G.—193rd. Pennsylvania Volunteers, I returned home, in the late part of November, and in the last call of President Lincoln, in February for volunteers to serve one year— during the war, I re-enlisted. In 1867 I went all through that campaign to the surrender of Lee at Appomattox. From appomattox we marched to intercept Gen. Johnston in N.C. and now I began to play a little more base-ball—

I started in as a pitcher of the Enterprise—then the leading club of Western Pennsylvania and in that year our regular team never lost but one game. In this same year I received my first salary as a base ball player. My salary amounting to the enormous sum of two dollars a week.

Old 'Deacon white' and I made the first glove ever used on the ball field, in 1870. Made from buck-skin driving glove. We were in N.Y. at the time. Whites hands were so sore he could not catch. We went down Broadway one day to a wholesale house and the only thing we could find suitable was a pair of heavy buck gauntlet gloves. We took these, cut the gauntlets off, cut the fingers out and took them to a tailors to put a little padding in the hand. We were playing the Mutuals of New York, and White came on the grounds with the gloves on. The crowd started to yell "take the gloves off,— take the gloves off" and the Mutuals protested to the umpires against White wearing the gloves. —The umpires decided that their was nothing in the rules to prohibit White from wearing the gloves, and Tim caught through the game although it took him some little time to get accustomed so he could hold the ball. It was not a great while until all the catchers were getting protection for their hands.

Ed Herrmann

(see p. 131 for typewrittten letter)

Moe Berg

(see p. 133 for typewritten letter)

Harry Danning

Dear Seth:

The Giants were playing in Boston, a day game, and after, Carl Hubbell, Mel Ott, Mark Koenig and myself decided to go to the Dog Track at Revere Beach—we took a train and arrived a little early for the track, so decided to go to the boardwalk at Revere—
While wandering through, we came upon a game—where a girl in a bathing suit sat on a piece of wood over a large vat of water—the object being if you hit the 'Bulls-Eye' the board would release and the girl would fall into the water—

I took my turn—Mel his, and Mark his and now it was Carl's turn—He hit the 'Bulls-eye' so many times in a row, that the poor girl quit and wouldn't sit on the board anymore—I think this story tells you more about the control that Carl had in his days in the majors—

Sincerely,

Harry

Milt May

1-10-97

Seth,

The pitcher was John 'the count' Montefusco

They were counting down on the scoreboard at Candlestick, the number of runs needed to the millionth. I understand they were doing that in all the ballparks. I, casually watched as the game went on and the number changed quickly 23 . . . 17 . . . 15 . . . etc. I was in the on deck circle and it was 7, 5 or something and Bob Watson hit a double. As I stepped into the batters box it clicked to one. The first pitch from John Montefusco was a low fastball and it went out. Bob Watson sprinted home accounting for the millionth run.

Evidently, Dave Concepcion hit a home run simultaneously with me and sprinted around the bases, but Bob, being on 2nd already, had the jump and scored seconds before.

Milt May

Paul Casanova

Dear Seth,

I was next to Tom House (relief pitcher) inside the bullpen. Tom caught the ball and we ran to home plate and gave Hank the ball. Times were very tough. Hank was receiving alot of death threats because he was black. We always had a security guard with us. One night in Alabama after an exhibition game against Baltimore the security guards told us we couldn't go outside our room because it wasn't safe. We waited a little while and sneaked out the back door and went to eat soul food. Luckily we ended up OK and nothing happen!

The next morning we arrived in Cincinatti to open the season with the Reds. I ran into Hank and his wife Billy outside the hotel and he told me "Casi, tomorrow I'm going to tie the record and the next day I'm going to sit out and wait till we get to Atlanta and break the record in the first game. So I get to have peace of mind the rest of the season!" In Cincinatti, I went inside the clubhouse to change my shirt and when I came outside Hank was running the bases. He had tied the record and I missed it!

In Atlanta he broke the record just like he said. He sat out the next day and the following day against the Dodgers he hit #716. I caught it Magnavox paid the Braves a million dollars for all the balls after #715.

Paul Casanova

Johnny Roseboro

11/12/98

We met about 10 years after the fight at Dodger Stadium, an old timers game.

He has become a very good friend.

John Roseboro

Juan Marichal

We talked a few times and he would tell me how to hold the ball to throw his curves. We shared pitching tips every time we would meet or just talk baseball. We have kept in touch through the years, bumping into each other at the Legends of Baseball Circuit as well as at the Hall of Fame Induction ceremonies in Cooperstown, New York.

Because I knew I was pitching against the best and against the Dodgers, that was a team I loved pitching against—because there was always a big crowd and a lot of rivalry between the Giants and the Dodgers.

Juan Marichal

Maury Wills

Juan Marichal was truly tough for me to steal off. The reason was because he changed his rhythm with consistency. He became tough to "time," and thereby keeping me from getting the jump I wanted. However, I got him anyhow!

Larry Jackson was even tougher, yet I tied and broke Ty Cobb's single-season record against him, numbers 96 and 97. The key for me was that I stole off the Giants' and Cardinal's catcher and middle infielders (delay steal to break Cobb's record).

Pitchers threw at my legs all the time! If they were going to put me on, they wanted me hurting. When not hurting, I immediately stole second and third (on the first two pitches) no matter what the score! Or thrown out trying! I felt defiant!

Maury Wills

Walter O'Malley

(see p. 143 for typewritten letter)

Danny McDevitt

(see p. 145 for typewritten letter)

Johnny Vander Meer

seth—

when warming up to start the game in Brooklyn. I played well when I heard the Great Brooklyn fans

Johnny Vander Meer

Dick Hall

I was experimenting with a knuckleball and it got away

One wild pitch—that knuckleball

Dick Hall

Marcia Haddix

Jan. 14, 1998

Dear Seth,

Most people assume the high-light of Harv's career was the twelve perfect inning game of May 26, 1959, but he wouldn't agree. He felt that game was a loss for his team and he didn't play to lose. Harv, being a team player, maintained the high-light of his career, without question, were the two games he won in the 1960 World Series.

There is no denying the twelve perfect inning game brought Harv lasting notoriety. He always wondered if it would have been as memorable to the public had he won the game!

When Harv was quite ill in Sept. 1991, we read in the newspapers that his Perfect Game was, after 32 years, suddenly declared not a Perfect Game. His friends, his fans, and former colleagues called and wrote to express their indignation. While Harv was comforted by the support he received, the satisfaction in his finest effort was never the same for him.

In his successes and in his failures. Harv was always a winner.

Sincerely,

Marcia Haddix

Mike Scott

I don't think the Mets wanted to go to a 7th game against the Astros that year anything can happen in a 7th game. The Met players were tough and very talented, but what made them special was their resiliency. They showed that in the series against the Astros and the Red Sox.

Mike Scott

Jack Lazorko

There is one game I'll always remember. It was a combination of hockey and pitching. We were playing the Milwaukee Brewers on a hot Sunday afternoon in Anaheim. I came up to the Big Leagues in 1984 and knew most of the players I was pitching against. They knew fielding was one of my strongest assets. Cecil Cooper hit two shots up the middle. I did the "splits" a hockey term for a goalie, and made a "kick" save early in the game, and a "glove" save later in the game.

I grew up in New Jersey playing hockey every winter between football and baseball season. I enjoyed playing goalie because it would quicken up my glove hand for baseball. I played third base all through high school.

Later in the game, Robin Yount and Paul Molitor hit balls up the middle and I made "glove" saves on both of them. As I turned to get the ball back from Jack Howell I saw all the infielders with their gloves underneath their arms. Dick Schofield yells "Hey Zork, we don't need our gloves anymore, we will just watch you play goalie."

Jack Lazorko

Eddie O'Brien

Seth:

In Spring Training (Ft. Meyers, Fla) we had split squads in the early going. John and I were in different groups. During one exebition game, He pinch-hit for Bob Friend in the third inning, changed to my number and pinch hit again in the 7th inning. This was the only time this happened, although we had opponents quite confused when we played basketball.

Sincerely

Ed O'Brien

P.S. He struck out for me!

Ron Reed

Seth,

In basketball you can have longevity if you can do one or two things well. For instance, being a great shooter, or a great rebounder, or a great ball handler. You have to do something well. I felt I didn't have the talent in any one thing to keep my N.B.A. career going very long. Only 11 or 12 players on an N.B.A. team, and every year the first round draft choice makes the team, and a lot of times the second or third round draft choice makes the team, the 'numbers' game can catch

up to a 'so-so' player rather quickly. If two new players are coming in the front door, two other players are going out the back door!

Ron Reed

Larry Gowell

(see p. 157 for typewritten letter)

Jim Colborn

Hi Seth—

The Brewers were pretty poor in the early 70's. In the bullpen we would even make up games where our team would be rewarded with a single for any foul ball, a double for a foul ball in the 2nd deck and a triple for a foul ball in the 3rd deck. A H.R. was either a foul ball past the foul pole or a foul over the top of the stadium. In any case we needed goofy stuff like that to stay sane while losing 90 games each year.

I guess that was my idea when I dressed up like the ground crew, visited Bernie Brewer in the beer mug or dressed up like an umpire. Dressing like an umpire was quite effective if I do say so myself. Jim Denkinger, the plate umpire as I recall, allowed me the loan of his chest protector and mask. It was the last day of the season and everyone was mostly interested in finishing the game and getting home. I guess we weren't too interested in little details like who was behind the umpire's mask. Alex Grammas, our manager, greeted Ralph Houk with, "You have a nice winter, Ralph." Ralph said, "You too, Alex." I chimed in, "You too, Alex." He half glanced at me, did a double take and bent over laughing. Our bench was loudly, verbally abusing the plate umpire, me, in hopes of getting tossed so they could head home early. I accomodated Ray Sadecki and Gorman Thomas but couldn't really figure out how to throw myself out as I wasn't on the bench.

Sincerely,

Jim Colborn

Jon Lieber

Dear Seth,

As far as studying each homeplate umpires strike zone? Me pearsonally, I think it is a good idea. Just for the fact you can get a feel for where he is going to be the most consistant in the strike zone.

We knew going into the season that we were going to be a team to compete with, no matter what anybody said. We felt like we've got nothing to lose. Everybody deep down inside, was very proud, not just of ourselfs, but as a team.

All my best Seth,

Jon Lieber #47

Pittsburgh Pirates

Milt Gaston

June 9, 1926

Mr B.B. Johnson

Chicago, Ill.

Sir:

Regarding the game of June 7th in this city during which I was alleged to have struck a spectator and for which I received a suspension I wish to state my case as follows:—

This fan had been riding me during the entire game, and after I was knocked from the box in the third inning he used abusive language and became personal. Because the way the game had gone I was hot-tempered enough to go into the stand, but only after he had dared me to do so. I could not say truthfully whether I hit said fan or not. I struck at him but it was mostly a battle of words. I realized my mistake a moment after I had entered the stands and left same when ordered to do so by the umpire; Mr. Rowland.

Respectfully yours

Milton Gaston

Bill Veeck

(see p. 164 for typewritten letter)

Charles Nagy

It seems like every game you have some relative or

friend in the stands watching the game. But when you are out there, they are the furthest thought in your mind. There are times when there are an unusual number, like in the play offs or when you play close to where you grew up, which might make you a little more nervous but like I said after the first pitch the game is all that is in your mind. About being on "center stage" as you put it, just do not look up. Focus on the catcher.

Monte Pearson

(see p. 167 for typewritten letter)

Jim Rooker

(see p. 169 for typewritten letter)

Zack Wheat

The 26 inn. game—it was quite a game—there was quite a few good players that kept the score down—also good pitching by both Cadore and Oeschger—If I rember right we jumped out of Boston that nite and played 17 inn. in Brooklyn the next day (Sun) went to Boston that nite and played there Mon. 19 inn. We lost both of those games—but that same year (1920) we won the pennant. I doubt if that game will ever be beat—but, records are to be broken & that one may beaten.

My best regards—

Sincerely

Zack Wheat

Marius Russo

Dear Seth,

Yes, I remember Lou Gehrig's speech that afternoon very well, Lou did an excellent job at the mike—His speech was heart-rending. All was still, not a sound anywhere. Both teams didn't miss a word. There were many tears. I remember especially Tony Lazzeri. Also Murphy and Gomez—Lou's teammates for many years, crying unabashedly.

When Babe Ruth embraced Gehrig, it made everyone happy and many smiles showed through wet eyes. The two great ballplayers. The greatest in our time.

Yes, Seth, I remember that day well. My rookie season—and I met so many good players, all the best.

Yours

Marius Russo

N.Y. Yankees

1939–'43, '46

Tommy Henrich

Seth

I am very honored to have been a good friend of Lou Gehrig.

He was extremely generous in giving me all the advice I asked for regarding pitchers I was to face for the first time.

He kidded me quite a bit. I felt very close to him because of it.

I played only the last two years with him but that was long enough for me to recognize what a belter he was.

He was a kind man but when he swung a bat he looked like he was swinging a tomahawk ready to kill the ball no matter where the pitcher threw it.

Bill Dickey and Lou were always together and I'm glad to say they were two of the greatest guys I ever met.

Sincerely

Tom

Jamie Moyer

May 9 1998

Seth:

The first part to your question about feeling alone is true. The mound is an 18 foot circle which I consider is my office. In my office my objective is to work together with my catcher through signs and both of our senses working together in sinc. My objective is to throw strikes, work fast, and utilize my defense. I do feel alone because ultimately I have the final say in what pitch is thrown. Which does have an effect on the outcome of the game. So it is important because my teamates fans, and myself have high expectations, of myself.

A pitcher has many thoughts while on the mound. Some of which can be fear, domination, intimidation, situations, counts, base-runners, location of pitches, memory of pitches thrown previously, how a hitter has had success or failure off of you, on deck hitter, tempo of oneself, and finally just getting hitters out. I feel the biggest thought is to stay positive with your thoughts and be aggressive. It doesn't matter whether you are a power pitcher or a finess pitcher. The object is to get the hitter out and allow your team to hit to score runs.

Jamie Moyer

Violet Whitehill Geissinger

Dear Seth:—

It was the end of the 1925 Baseball season and everyone was going home for the winter months. A good friend on the Detroit team, Harry [Heilmann], insisted I meet his friend Earl Whitehill. He knew I would like him. Harry [Heilmann] was also a good friend of Babe Ruth and his wife Claire. So Mrs. Ruth gave a lovely dinner party and Harry [Heilmann] brought Earl along, so we met!

When I was in New York I always stayed with

Claire and her mother and two brothers. This was before she and Babe married.

Yes, Earl Whitehill was a handsome man and I liked him very much. We all had a fun time that night. He wanted to know if I ever thought of getting married. Later I told him "Yes" I'll marry you Earl."

We had twenty seven years of marriage. Thank you again Seth. Just for being you.

Violet

Jean Faut

Dear Seth,

My favorite pastime growing up in a small town which was fortunate to host a semi-pro baseball team was practicing with that team every evening. A few of those players taught me all the pitches. I pitched an exhibition game with them, or I should say I made an appearance.

When the All American Girls Professional Baseball League (AAGPBL) switched from underhanded pitching to overhand, I was 'home free.' I developed my excellent control by throwing stones a long distance at telephone poles by the hour in the alley behind my home. Never realizing how valuable that experience would be a few years later.

The eight years I played in the AAGPBL were the most memorable years of my life. To follow your dream is the greatest accomplishment you can experience.

Sincerely,

Jean

Bill Voiselle

On 9/6/96 the town of "96" honored 'ole 96. A picture of 'ole 96 hangs in the town welcoming center. Yes, this town has honored me.

The jersey I kept until a few years ago, sold it to a big Atlanta fan.

Bill Voiselle

Larry Yount

I know you had to dig deep to find out about me, so I'll get the story right for you, and then a couple of thoughts.

I was called up in late 1971 from the minors and was called into the game to pitch. Being 21, I knew before going to the mound that my elbow was in pain, but figured that the excitement of the moment would make the pain go away. Warming up on the mound I actually used good judgement and pulled myself before I really got hurt. The following year after a great spring training I was sent to the minors, never to return to the major leagues.

Thoughts

1. If I ever thought that would be my only opportunity to pitch in the major leagues, I would have done so.

2. I would have faced Henry Aaron

3. To this day I can't believe I was not a successful pitcher in the major leagues.

4. I was able to accomplish about a 120% of my business ability and only 80% of my athletic ability.

5. I now have a great family and could not be much happier, except that void of not accomplishing my boyhood dreams.

Bert Blyleven

Dear Seth,

Wish I could have pitched until I die.

Good luck in life,

Bert

Waite Hoyt

(see p. 186 for typewritten letter)

PHOTOGRAPHY CREDITS

Baseball Hall of Fame Library

Enough cannot be said about the time and effort Bill Burdick from the Hall of Fame Photography archives put into this project. Thank you, Bill, for offering me so many great photographs to choose from.

Carl Pavano (Brian Spurlock, photographer)

Cy Young

Carl Mays

Reggie Jackson

Jim Palmer

Vic Raschi (picture of Casey Stengel)

Dickie Kerr

Joe Jackson

Kenesaw Mountain Landis

Chet Hoff

Walter Johnson

Satchel Paige

Jose Lima (Steve Schwab, photographer)

Ed Herrmann

Maury Wills

Al Schacht

Brown Brothers

Chet Hoff (of stadium)

Marius Russo (photo of Lou Gehrig hitting a baseball)

The Sporting News Archives

A sincere thank-you to Steve Gietschier for his efforts and expertise.

Al Hrabosky

Curt Schilling

Dutch Ruether

C. J. Nitkowski

Rocky Colavito

Eddie O'Brien

Bill Voiselle

Keystone Photo

Violet Geissinger

Photographs used courtesy of Major League Baseball

Mike Torrez

Jack Lazorko

Chan Ho Park

Rolando Arrojo

Pete Harnisch

Justin Thompson

Terry Collins

Charles Nagy

AP/Worldwide Photo

Thank you, Holly Jones, for your time and help.

Kerry Wood

Roger Clemens

Steve Carlton

Turk Wendell

Pedro Martinez

Jeff Bagwell

David Cone

Tom Glavine

Jaret Wright (Charles Krupa, photographer)

Christy Mathewson

Stu Miller

Don Liddle

Johnny Vander Meer

"Bleacher Entrance" frontispiece photograph

UPI/Corbis-Bettmann

Thank you to Norman Currie for his help.

Dizzy Dean

Don Newcombe

Bill Lee

Barry Halper (photo of Jimmie Foxx)

Lefty Grove

Jim Bouton

Carl Hubbell

Les Mueller (picture of Pete Gray)

Marius Russo (photo of Gehrig giving speech)

Bert Blyleven

Gary Kroll (The Beatles)

Moe Berg

Johnny Roseboro

The State Journal Register

Hub Kittle

Brace Photo

Thank you again, Mary and George.

Mace Brown (himself)

Jerry Reuss

Vic Raschi (himself)

Pete Rose

Max Lanier

"Blue Moon" Odom

Robin Roberts

Art Ditmar

Milt May

Dave Campbell

Les Mueller

Marcia Haddix (photo of Harvey Haddix)

Monte Stratton

Marius Russo

Brooklyn Public Library

Danny McDevitt

Pittsburgh Post Gazette

Jim Rooker (Derrell Sapp, photographer)

Transcendental Graphics

Thank you to Mark Rucker.

Mace Brown (Babe Ruth photo)

Maury Wills (photo of Juan Marichal)

Luis Tiant

Zack Wheat

All documents and memorabilia in *Every Pitcher*

Tells a Story courtesy of the Seth Swirsky collection.

BIBLIOGRAPHY

The Baseball Encyclopedia. 10th ed. New York: Macmillan, 1996.

Dewey, Donald, and Nicholas Acocella. *The Biographical History of Baseball*. New York: Carroll & Graf, 1995.

The Editors of *Sporting News*. *Baseball*. New York: Galahad Books, 1993.

Light, Jonathan Fraser. *The Cultural Encyclopedia of Baseball*. Jefferson, N.C.: McFarland & Company, 1997.

Lyons, Jeffrey, and Douglas B. *Out of Left Field*. New York: Times Books, 1998.

Thorne, John, and Pete Palmer with David Reuther. *Total Baseball*. 2nd ed. New York: Warner Books, 1991.

ACKNOWLEDGMENTS

I want to acknowledge those people who took time out of their busy lives to help with the creation of *Every Pitcher Tells a Story*.

Philip Turner, my editor, who looks for reasons to say yes instead of no. And all the dedicated people at Times Books—especially Carie Freimuth, Chad Bunning, Mary Beth Roche, Kate Larkin, and Angela Retino—for their belief in and support of this project.

My tireless assistants, Eva Fischer and Jennifer Hall, who did *all* of the little things which are always the big things. What was life like before you?

John T. Bird, of the Birmingham, Alabama Birds, for letting me bounce it all off him.

A million thank-you's: Dr. Laurel Anderson, Dave Aust, Jeff Balash, Marty Bandier, Mrs. Betty Barker, Tyler Barnes, Dave Baudoin, Matt Bialer, Jack Berke, Jeff Brown, Bari Buckner Quattro, Mary Anne Campos, Orestes Chavez, Tony Cocci, Eliot Runyan, Dottie Collins, Allen Courtney, Mark Gimpel, Susie Giuliani, Billy "N" Goldberg, Dorene Gordon, Roger Greenawalt ("Heather" lives!), Mike Gutierrez, Alan Hendricks, Josephine Impostato, Kip Ingle, Joey Klein, Evan Lamberg, Andrew Levy, Byrdie Lifson Pompan, P. J. Loyello, J. T. Miller, Carmen Molina, Susan Nalti, Elsie Nunez, John Olguin, John Ondrosek, Ethan Orlinsky, Paul Reiferson, Darci Ross, Mike Samson, Jeff Sanders, Joan Scheibel, Richie Scheinblum, Kevin Shea, Mike Sheehan, Greg Simm, Darrell Simon, Rick Solomon, Jimmy Spence, David Stephen, Steve Stout, Bart Swain, Joan Swirsky, Hank Thomas, Leigh Tobin, Jim Trdinich, David Tuttle, Rick Vaughn, Mike Veeck, Les Wolff, Eric Zohn, and Arnold, Eric, and Sean at Copies Unlimited in the Valley.

To Jody, I love you.
And to my beautiful slugger Julian—who's my boy?

Much love to my mother and father, Joan and Steve Swirsky. Also, to my grandma Mimi, Gertrude Krevit Finkle—at 86, a continuing inspiration to me. Finally, always in my memory, my grandfather Joel Finkle, my uncle Zachary Finkle, my great-grandmother Bubbe Fanny, my grandparents Ruth and Barney Swirsky, and my father-in-law Charles Gerson.

Finally, and most important, thank you to all the people who wrote letters in this book for allowing us to share your experiences.

Pitcher Dizzy Dean blows his horn, 1934.

ABOUT THE AUTHOR

Seth Swirsky grew up in Great Neck, New York, and graduated from Dartmouth College. He is a songwriter who has written for such artists as Celine Dion, Al Green, and Tina Turner. "Tell It To My Heart" and "Prove Your Love," both sung by Taylor Dayne, were worldwide top ten hits. His songs have earned him over twenty-one gold and platinum records. One of his new songs, "Instant Pleasure," is featured in the movie *Big Daddy*. As a record producer, he has recorded such artists as Faith Evans and Peter Allen. A lifelong baseball fan, Swirsky is the author of *Baseball Letters: A Fan's Correspondence with His Heroes*, about which Yogi Berra said, "It ain't over till it's over . . . and I never wanted Baseball Letters to be over." Swirsky's collection of baseball memorabilia may be viewed at www.sethsroom.com. He enjoys painting and writing poetry. Seth Swirsky lives in Beverly Hills, California, with his wife, Jody Gerson, and their five-year-old son Julian.

"The Clown Prince of Baseball," Al Schacht.

EVERY PITCHER
TELLS A STORY